CHANGES FOR THE BETTER

Reprinted from 'Old & Young in Elizabeth's Days'
and other articles

by

G. M. ALEXANDER

with slight additions

Volume 1

ZOAR PUBLICATIONS
44 Queen's Drive, Ossett,
W. Yorks. WF5 0ND.

1976

ISBN 0 904435 12 1

ACKNOWLEDGEMENTS

The publishers desire to express their deep gratitude to the relatives of the late G. M. Alexander for their ready permission to reprint from her book 'Old and Young in Elizabeth's Days'; in their editing of this material to Mr. K. W. H. Howard of Stamford for his ready and frequent help; to Miss Pauline Smith of Southampton University for some of the illustrations; and to Mr. Timothy Abbott who has so ably executed the time charts and maps that form such an integral part of the present edition.   D.O.

Printed in Great Britain by
O. & M. Ltd., 1 Rugby Street, Leicester, LE3 5FF

CONTENTS

	Page
MARION FAIRLEY	1
THE COLD NIGHT IN PONTELAND	7
THE UNGRATEFUL PUPIL	11
GEOFFREY HURST'S TROUBLE	17
BOLD ROTHWELL	25
THE STATELY HOMES OF ENGLAND	29
THE NOBLE HOUSE OF HUNTINGDON	41
FOXE'S BOOK OF MARTYRS	57
JOHN DAY THE PRINTER	63
THE FIRE AND THE PESTILENCE	71
MR. GREENHAM'S HARVEST	77
ARCHBISHOP GRINDAL AND THE PROPHESYINGS	85
WILLIAM PERKINS	97
JOHN PRESTON'S CHANGE	105
JOHN PRESTON'S FRIEND	109
POOR MR. BAINS	113
RICHARD BLACKERBY	117
SIR NATHANIEL AND NOVEMBER 5th	123
MR. FAIRCLOUGH'S LAMBS	129
SIR SAMUEL'S LETTERS	133

	1520	1540	1560	1580	1600	1620	1640	1660	1680
HENRY VIII			E	M	ELIZABETH I		JAMES I	CHARLES I	O.C	CHARLES II

PAUL BAINS

N.BARNARDISTON

S.BARNARDISTON ▶

RICHARD BLACKERBY

W.BRADSHAW

THOMAS CARTWRIGHT

LAURENCE CHADDERTON

HUGH CHOMELEY

JOHN COTTON

JOHN DAY

SAMUEL FAIRCLOUGH

JOHN FOXE

T.GATAKER

ANTHONY GILBY

BERNARD GILPIN

RICHARD GREENHAM

EDMUND GRINDAL

JOSEPH HALL

ARTHUR HILDERSHAM

EARL OF HUNTINGDON

GEOFFREY HURST

W.PERKINS

JOHN PRESTON

RICHARD ROTHWELL

W.VEITCH ▶

| 1520 | 1540 | 1560 | 1580 | 1600 | 1620 | 1640 | 1660 | 1680 |

The principal characters

Marion Fairley

ONE day, when my sister and I were in Edinburgh for a holiday, we saw the name "The Braids" on one of the city trams. "Oh" I thought, " 'Fairley of the Braids' is one of the men we read of as a friend of the great John Knox." So we took that tram-ride and found ourselves on golf links. "Only golf links," I thought. I had been looking forward to seeing some ancient mansion, or even only its ruin, the seat of "the ancient family of the Fairleys of the Braids".

The golf links may certainly have been very old; they played golf in Scotland long before they did so in England; in fact, in the old days when bows and arrows were used in war, woe betide those men and youths who played golf instead of practising with their bows and arrows; it was forbidden for a time. But when guns came in, archery, with the use of the bow, gradually became only play, like golf, and golf looked up again. I do not, however, know in the slightest when golf was first played on the Braids. All *I* know is about Marion Fairley "of the ancient family of the House of Braid", and about her great-grandfather.

One Sabbath day, the 16th November 1572, Robert Fairley of Braid did not go home to dinner from the kirk in Edinburgh. The great Reformer John Knox was lying on his deathbed in that house at the top of the Canongate, and he went to see him. A little dinner was brought for Knox to take (perhaps broth made the day before, and a morsel of mealy pudding made many weeks before, and hung up in its skin in the kitchen). Knox said, "But this is the Fast Day, we are not eating to-day." What Fast Day did he mean? The Spanish Armada was coming, with its "slavery-dooming ships", to

JOHN KNOX
returning home after having preached his last sermon

'Having finished the service, and pronounced the blessing with a cheerful but exhausted voice, he came down from the pulpit, and leaning upon his staff crept down the street, which was lined with the audience who, as if anxious to take the last sight of their beloved pastor, followed him until he entered his house, from which he never again came out alive.'   McCrie's *Life of Knox.*

subdue England and Scotland to the tyranny of the Pope. The ships were full of torture-weapons. The Scots had appointed a day for humiliation before God, to beseech Him in prayer, to deliver them from their great enemy. That was the work of that day; hearty meals would lead to drowsiness; now let them avoid them and give themselves unto prayer. When Knox mentioned the Fast Day, Robert Fairley reminded him that the next Sabbath, not that one, was the day appointed. And oh the thousands of heartfelt prayers and cries that went up that next Sabbath, that the Lord of hosts would appear on behalf of the Protestants. And we know how they were answered 16 years later in 1588: the time came when those ships were lying wrecked round the coasts of Britain.

On this day, however, they brought dinner up for Robert Fairley. He took it at a little table beside the bed, and Knox, seeing that he had made a mistake, had some too.

It was the custom in those days to allow many friends to come to the bedsides of dying men, and the next week did not pass without lords, great statesmen, ministers, elders, deacons and private friends, visiting Knox. On Thursday Robert Fairley went again and his hope was to be the last visitor left in the room with Knox. When he rode home along the quiet dark roads to the Braids, his mind and heart were full of Knox's kind last words to him. For when they were alone Knox had said, "I have been greatly indebted to you, I shall never be able to recompense you, but I commit you to One who is able to do it—to the Eternal God."

That may be read in McCrie's *Life of Knox*. All that generation passed away, and the next passed away, and in the

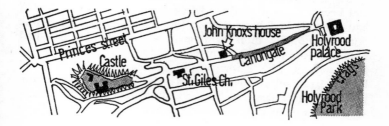

third generation lived the father of Marion Fairley. Marion was born in the year 1638. Her parents did not live at the Braids but in Lanark. They brought her up 'in the nurture and admonition of the Lord'. Every morning and every evening, mother, children and servants were assembled while Marion's father led the singing of a psalm, and read the Bible and prayed. Their minister Mr. Birnie, preached about Jesus Christ, and when he came to their house Marion sometimes heard them all talking together about God. They spoke as if they loved God. Marion felt that she did not know Him, but that she would have to know Him if she ever went to heaven. Her parents never forgot that Robert Fairley of Braid, her father's grandfather, had been committed in prayer to the Eternal God by His servant John Knox. Their own chief prayers for themselves and their children were that He would be their eternal Refuge.

One day when Marion was quite a big girl, she knelt down in her bedroom and prayed to God for His blessing on her soul. Then she went downstairs to her mother. Someone had come in, and was reading aloud a letter that looked as if it had been read and read, and folded up again, often. And it had been; it had been written the year before Marion was born. A notable minister named Samuel Rutherford had written it to a man whose name was John Gordon. John had been one of Mr. Rutherford's congregation, but a cruel bishop had had Rutherford sent away and kept in prison, just as Satan's servants have so often done. He was really very happy in prison even although it was cold there, and he far away from home. He was happy because Jesus made him feel that He loved him and had forgiven all his sins. He often thought about the people who used to sit listening while he preached, and John was one of them. Mr. Rutherford did not know whether John ever thought about God and about his own soul or not. He thought perhaps he forgot all about Jesus and heaven and hell, the minute he got out of the building. Marion did not hear the beginning of the letter but there were very solemn things all through it. Mr. Rutherford said that many people make a start to go to heaven but they give it over because the devil sets a sweet-smelling flower to their noses—i.e. this pleasant world, and they are so bewitched and charmed with it that they forget that another world, heaven or hell, is before them. He said that many are like Esau or Judas or Balaam or Saul or Pharaoh or Simon Magus or Caiaphas or Ahab, who all seemed on some of the days in their lives as if now they were going to be good men, and yet after all they were not God's children. Pharaoh and Simon Magus asked God's people to pray for them, but they had no love to them or to God after all. Mr. Rutherford was afraid that John Gordon was perhaps like one of them.

When Marion heard the letter, she became very much afraid that *she* would turn out to be like Esau or Saul or one of the others. She went about often thinking "Oh I shall go to hell". But one day the words came to her mind, "To whom, Lord, shall we go? Thou hast the words of eternal life," and another day the words "Those that seek Me early shall find Me." Oh she *did* like them. The Holy Ghost had sent them into her heart, to make her stop thinking she would

1570	1580	1590	1600	1610	1620	1630	1640	1650
Elizabeth I				James I		Charles I		
Knox's prayer								
								Marion
				Rutherford's letter				

go to hell, and make her feel there was a Saviour, Jesus, and she would go to Him and she would find Him. It was a *change for the better*.

And often through her life, when she was in trouble, God sent words from the Bible into her very soul, and in the end took her to heaven.

I should think when you read "Marion Fairley" at the top you thought there would be some interesting little stories about Marion. Perhaps, if you have read any of it, you thought you would not go on any further, because you saw the words "heaven" and "hell" and "God's people" in it. Well, if we had been in the Garden of Eden, we would all have hidden ourselves, like Adam and Eve, from the presence of the Lord God, amongst the trees of the garden. It is our nature. But God gives His people another nature as well. He says "Where art thou?" to them and leads them to love Him, and not turn away from everything He loves.

Marion, when she grew up, became the wife of William Veitch.

Now I will just let you have a peep at the last bit of Rutherford's letter to John Gordon of Rusco, that Marion heard being read:

'I recommend Christ and his love to you, in all things. Let him have the flower of your heart and your love. Set a low price upon all things but Christ; and cry down, in your thoughts, clay and dirt, that will not comfort you, when ye get summons to remove, and appear before your Judge, to answer for all the deeds done in the body. The Lord give you wisdom in all things. I beseech you to sanctify God in your speaking, for holy and reverend is his name: and be temperate and sober: fondness of too much company is a sin that holds men out of heaven.'

The Cold Night in Ponteland

NOW comes a story about this man of God, William Veitch, some years later, when he was taken to prison as Peter and John and Paul and Silas were, just because they followed Christ; and about the good man's poor wife Marion, left alone with the children, but also about the wicked man who had caused all their trouble. It *had* been an upsetting night for her when the soldiers came to the house to take her husband to prison. She said, "It bred some new trouble and fear to my spirit; but He was graciously pleased to set home that word 'He does all things well'; 'Trust in the Lord, and fear not what man can do'; which brought peace to me in such a measure that I was made to wonder; for all the time the officers were in the house, He supported me so that I was not in the least discouraged before them." But they took her husband away to prison because of his faithful preaching. And the time of the story was in the year 1680, about three hundred years ago.

All that northern region near Newcastle and up to Berwick, was in what used to be known as the Border Land. For ages the English on one side and the Scots on the other had had fierce disputes and fights. But in the year 1680 these had long ceased and the two countries had one king.

Sometime after her husband had been imprisoned Mrs. William Veitch (Marion) was one day riding on horseback from her home in Longhorsley to Morpeth. A man-servant was with her. The month was January; there was a blinding snowstorm; her husband lay in Morpeth jail; she had had a letter from him that day asking her to come and see him, for

1640	1650	1660	1670	1680	1690	1700	1710	1720
Charles I		OC	Charles II		J	W+M	Anne	George
William Veitch				prison		buried together		
				MR. MRS. VEITCH				
Marion Fairley								

on the morrow he was to be sent to Edinburgh. She might never see him again; the great ones might put him to death, with just the same hatred to him in their hearts as Ahab had to Micaiah*, and the Scribes and Pharisees had to the Lord Jesus.

They rode on and on and on and on, snow all the way to Morpeth. They reached the prison at midnight. The guards said that Mrs. Veitch would have to wait till morning before she could see her husband. And so she sat by the fire, till clankings and voices let her know that the day's work had begun. She was allowed to speak to her husband, but soldiers were in the room all the time. He was led away to a prison in Edinburgh. "Then," she said, "I went to a friend's house in the town and wept my fill, and some friends with me."

But she had been strengthened in this journey by the words in the eighth chapter of Isaiah: "Neither fear ye their fear nor be afraid. Sanctify the Lord of Hosts Himself and let Him be your fear, and let Him be your dread."

The Vicar of Longhorsley, Thomas Bell, had always hated Mrs. Veitch. He was a parson who drank and swore, as many did in those days. It was he who had soldiers sent to Mr. Veitch's house to capture and imprison him. On that snowy day, he had said, "Now Veitch will be hanged to-morrow as he deserves."

That week Vicar Bell left Newcastle to go home. Knowing the curate of Ponteland, he called on him on his way. They sat talking and drinking till 10 o'clock, when Mr. Bell said he must be going home. The night was dark and cold and

* I Kings 22, 8.

the curate said the River Pont (which he would have to cross) was swollen. But Mr. Bell had his way, for though the curate had locked up his horse in the stable, he forced him to let him have it and went away. He did not reach home, nor even leave Ponteland. Two days after they found his dead body in the river, in a standing position and up to the arms in ice— *one solid block of ice.*

"Who can stand before His cold?" the psalmist asked in the one hundred and forty-seventh psalm. "He giveth snow like wool, He scattereth the hoarfrost like ashes. He casteth forth His ice like morsels: who can stand before His cold?"

The people who loved Mr. Veitch and mourned that he was shut up in prison, said that this was a judgment from God upon the wicked persecutor. It was so. They said to Mrs. Veitch that now nobody would trouble Mr. Veitch again. But she said that if the other enemies round about would not take heed to God's warnings in the Bible, they would not because of that take warning either. The words kept occurring to her mind, "Rejoice not when thine enemy falleth". Mr. Veitch was at length freed, and they lived together till 1722, and died at a good old age and were buried together on the same day in the town of Dumfries. Many lovely stories were told, long ago, by a good minister, Mr. James Anderson. He took them from Mrs. Veitch's diary and they are "kindly handed down to us".

I will just tell you one more story. In those days of persecution, Mr. Veitch was obliged for a time to escape to Holland,

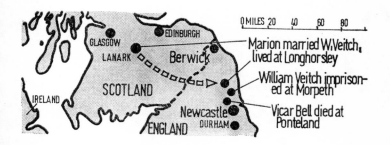

and Mrs. Veitch sent the two eldest boys to him over there. But then their third boy, who was only twelve, was very seriously ill, and she realised he would not get better. She was troubled, wondering most of all if her boy really belonged to Jesus Christ. How she prayed the Lord to show her for certain whether her boy's soul was saved.

One day he called her to the side of his bed, and told her he had given up thinking about the world. How was that? He said, "I have seen another sight! I have been praying, and giving myself to Christ, and he answered me that he took pleasure in my soul, which has comforted me." He often exclaimed after that, "Whom have I in heaven but thee, and whom desire I in the earth besides thee?" (Psalm 73.25). His mother felt more refreshed by all this than if he had been made heir of a large estate. After this, he only seemed to want to talk about better things, and either to pray himself, or to hear others pray. When in the end he could not speak, he held up his hand when his mother spoke to him of death and heaven, and 'so', his mother writes, 'we parted, in hope of a glorious meeting.'

The Ungrateful Pupil

In the early days of Queen Elizabeth I, as Bernard Gilpin, the 'Apostle of the North', was walking towards Oxford, he saw before him a boy who sometimes ran and sometimes walked. The 'apostle' at last overtook him and asked where he was going. "To Oxford," said the boy; and to make a long story short, their meeting ended in Bernard Gilpin's taking the boy home with him, putting him to school, and later sending him to the University, paying the fees which he could not afford himself.

You will wonder why he was called the Apostle of the North. The people in the north of England were sunk in darkness, knew nothing of the Bible or of the true God and Jesus Christ, just as the heathen had been when Paul and the other apostles went to them over all the known world, and preached. To these people Bernard Gilpin preached and God blessed them; from being ignorant papists and bad-living people, many became godly. Dr. Gilpin had preached before King Edward VI, and his relatives were powerful with the new Queen. She would have made him Bishop of Carlisle if he had been willing to accept the office; but he thought God had called him rather to stay with the people at Houghton for the most part, and not to go to Carlisle. He determined to spend all his time, strength and money for the good of as many people as he could. He prayed earnestly to God to bless his preaching to the people of the wild moors. It had already been blessed to his flock at Houghton in Queen Mary's reign, and his return to them at her death was "through crowds of joyful people."

There is a well-known story about him. He was very fond of those blessed words, "All things work together for good to them that love God, to them who are the called according to

1510	1520	1530	1540	1550	1560	1570	1580	1590
	Henry VIII			E.	M.	Elizabeth	I	
			Preached before King ■		■	Heresy charge	■	Bishop's summons
		BERNARD GILPIN						

His purpose," and he often used to quote them. On that memorable journey to London to be tried for his life he broke his leg. Some mockingly asked him if he imagined that that would work for his good. "Yes," said Bernard, "all things." And so it turned out; the broken leg meant that he could not go on with the journey, but had to remain in an inn, and so never reached London, never reached the prison, never reached the cruel stake, for news arrived that Queen Mary had died. So he returned home to Houghton-le-Spring near Durham, and there he lived and was a blessing till the day of his death, 4th March 1583, nearly a quarter of a century later.

Dr. Gilpin in his life-time had so much money coming to him from family property that he employed an almoner to give away a great deal of it and spend it on good uses. The almoner's name was William Airey. Gilpin might have enjoyed great luxury at home, but at Christmas time he would say, "Now William, you and I must be getting ready for our journey;" and away they would ride on their horses to a dreadful part of the country called The Debateable Land, on the border of England and Scotland. There the people were particularly savage and superstitious. They would swear "by the mass" and "by our lady," and believed that the priest could save their souls. They were robbers and thieves; they carried off each other's cattle, stabbed each other in the dark, and burned to the ground the barns of their enemies. They could be hospitable in a barbarous way, and kind to their friends; their halls would resound with drunken merriment at Christmas time. But they were fierce and wild. The gospel had never been preached in The Debateable Land till Bernard Gilpin went there. He chose Christmas time because they kept Christmas, and he could find them at leisure for that season.

BERNARD GILPIN

So in driving snow he and William Airey would urge their horses on. When night fell they were sometimes far from home or dwelling, and Gilpin would say, "Walk the horses up and down, William, here, while we can still see it is a road track." So all night William would trot the horses backwards and forwards, while he himself would pace the road close by, flapping his arms and exercising himself one way or another till the morning light showed them where they could ride on safely. The rest offered them was not luxurious nor the food delicate, but weariness and hunger made them welcome. There was a gravity and majesty about this holy man of God that struck the rude Borderers, and soon they began to look upon him as a prophet. In some old church or great spacious barn, he would preach and preach and preach again, and great numbers flocked to hear him.

I wonder if you have forgotten the boy he overtook on the way to Oxford, or have wondered what became of him. He was one of many thus befriended. Gilpin had founded and endowed a Grammar School in Houghton-le-Spring, and kept many of the boys in a school-house at his own charge. If they loved learning he sent them to the University and sometimes visited them there. That particular boy was very good at languages but apt to be quarrelsome. But Dr. Gilpin continued his kindness to the boys whether they were perfect or not. The school became famous; rich men sent their sons to it, and as the parsonage was wide and rambling they boarded there as well as at the schoolhouse. The larders and butteries of both houses were equally well stocked from the rich pastures of the glebe.

Many learned men visited the school, among them Cecil, Lord Burghley. According to the account he evidently went away with feelings like those of the Queen of Sheba when she saw the glories of Solomon. It was however not kingly glory he saw, but rather the true glory of a bishop, for a bishop must be "given to hospitality, apt to teach" (1 Timothy 3. 2); and though his great friend Pilkington was really the Bishop of Durham, the Apostle of the North was in his manner of life a true bishop: "holding fast the faithful word, given to hospitality," and allowing no poor man to be turned from his door. People from the whole region round constantly came to him for help or good counsel, and were kept to dine or have supper with him, or spend a night, a week, or a month as their need might be.

But the time came when this good man got into trouble with Bishop Pilkington's successor, Dr. Barnes. Someone stirred him up against him, and he said angrily, "I will hear him preach." He sent a message requiring him to preach at a certain place. Gilpin was just about to set out for The Debateable Land, and not knowing the Bishop's angry feelings, sent a respectful excuse. When he returned from his tour in the dales of the Border it was to learn that he had been suspended from preaching and was forbidden to preach even in his own pulpit. This grieved him; how could it do otherwise? especially when he heard that the Bishop had been led to dislike him through something that had been said by—whom? By that very boy, now at college, whom he had overtaken, running and walking, on the road! So the little verse, written in those days, was true to Dr. Gilpin:

> "Blow, blow, thou winter wind,
> Thou art not so unkind
>   As man's ingratitude;
> Thy tooth is not so keen,
> Because thou art not seen,
>   Although thy breath be rude."

One day soon after that sad time, Gilpin was summoned to meet the Bishop at Chester-le-Street near Durham. He went not knowing what the Bishop would say to him; but one thing he knew—that "all things work together for good to them that love God." What the Bishop said on seeing him was, "Sir, I must have you preach today." Gilpin was unprepared, yet preached a long sermon. He noticed a secretary sitting by with pen in hand to write down what he said. Before his sermon ended, a spirit of great fearlessness was given him. He turned to the Bishop saying that now it was to him he must preach. Place after place in his diocese was still sunk in ignorance and popery, and God would require

O MILES 20   40   60   80

Gilpin's preaching tours of
'The Debateable Land'

Gilpin preached before
Bishop at Chester-le-Street

Gilpin preacher at
Houghton-le-Spring

GLASGOW EDINBURGH
LANARK
BERWICK
SCOTLAND ENGLAND
NEWCASTLE
Carlisle Durham

an account of his work. He could not say, "Behold, I knew it not!"—a shepherd must feed his flock. With many such solemn warnings the preacher continued, the listeners sitting astonished for he "thundered it out."

Afterwards at dinner in an inn his friends anxiously expressed their care for his safety, for an offended bishop frequently sent his clergy to prison. He told them not to fear seeing God overrules everything. "But you have to see the Bishop again," they said. "Yes," he replied, "I must go to take leave of him," and so saying he made his way to the Bishop. Dr. Barnes rose from his chair and said, "Dr. Gilpin, I will go home with you." And so, says the writer of the story, he went along with him to his house and walking there together in a parlour, he took him by the hand and asked his forgiveness, saying that Gilpin was more fit to be Bishop of Durham than he himself was to be the parson at Houghton-le-Spring. He promised him too that no one should injure him with his good-will as long as he was bishop.

So once again Gilpin found that all things had worked together for his good, and he was still able to keep his doors open for the poor, to educate his boys, and to preach to and teach his own flock at Houghton-le-Spring, and the countrymen in the dark dales of Northumbria.

That wonderful verse has been called Bernard Gilpin's Motto. How beautiful it is that it was given to one of God's servants at "the beginning of days" in England, after the night of the rule of the Pope of Rome had passed away! How often from that time to the present the cause of God in England has seemed to be almost broken down—almost at the door of a prison of darkness such as Spain is in; and yet the saints of God continue to find to this very day that "all things work together for good to them that love God, to them who are the called according to His purpose."

Geoffrey Hurst's Trouble

THE life and labours of Bernard Gilpin give us a picture of the day of prosperity in the spread of the gospel, and indeed much might be added to that picture without exaggerating the amount of good that came in with Queen Elizabeth. The very bonfires that blazed and crackled on the night of the 18th of November, 1558, purifying the air from the infection of a recent fever, while they celebrated the Queen's accession, might have been regarded as symbolising the purification of the land from popery.

A quotidian ague or typhus fever had raged for four months; thirteen bishops, persecutors more or less, and a thousand people had died of it that autumn. Now it was over. Soon, too, bonfires were kindled for another purpose—to burn crucifixes! How eagerly the Londoners ran with these from St. Paul's Cathedral to Smithfield and burnt *them there*! How soon Edward VI's prayer was heard in the churches, "From the tyranny of the Bishop of Rome and all his detestable enormities, good Lord deliver us!" And protestant exiles came from abroad; some preachers came from their hiding-places in England, the Service was conducted in English instead of Latin and the Bible was read aloud chapter by chapter. Men strongly on the side of the Reformation were elected to Parliament. A public disputation was appointed to discuss true and false doctrines, and as the mass-priests did not offer to defend their favourite dogma they were brought low in the eyes of their own people.

But "trouble trod upon relief." It was impossible but that offences should come.

Now there was a man named Geoffrey Hurst, who like Bernard Gilpin had escaped martyrdom through the death of Queen Mary, and who rejoiced in these early signs of

1490	1500	1510	1520	1530	1540	1550	1560	1570
Henry VII		Henry VIII				E M	Elizabeth	
		approx. ▼			Brother-in-law martyred ■	■ ■	Act of Uniformity	
		GEOFFREY HURST						

better things, singing with many an Englishman in those days the song of Moses: "Thou shalt bring them in, and plant them in the mountain of Thine inheritance, in the place, O Lord, which Thou hast made for Thee to dwell in." But, while Gilpin travelled on like Joshua or Caleb, and possessed some of the fields and hills of Canaan, Geoffrey went only a little way beyond the waters of Marah. His whole life indeed had been a troublous one, and before going forward with him from his deliverance on to that Marah, we will go back and see something of what he had suffered under the Egyptians.

He was a brother-in-law of George Marsh, a martyr who was burnt at Chester. He lived near Pennington in Lancashire, but hunted by the priests in the days of the persecution he used to leave his wife and little family and go into Yorkshire where he was not known. He was a nailer but whether or not he made and sold nails while in Yorkshire I do not know. He had hardships but did not starve, and neither did his little ones at home. Sometimes he stole back to his home by night to comfort his poor wife, and on those occasions he usually took with him some good minister who might also have been arrested and imprisoned had not the Lord hidden him. During their sojourn under Geoffrey's roof, sixteen or twenty, and sometimes twenty-four people would meet furtively by night and the minister would preach. In this way the little company had the ministrations of no fewer than four Yorkshire clergymen—Mr. Best, Mr. Brown, Mr. Reneses and Mr. Russell. It was not safe however for Geoffrey to be at home, and before long the two faithful men would betake themselves, again by night, to their hiding place in Yorkshire.

And so Geoffrey Hurst went on, until after a long time a Justice of the Peace, Judge Lelond, and a priest Ralph Parkinson, actually did find him at home and cited him to appear at court in Lancaster to answer for his heresy and, of course, to be burnt. Four days after that, Queen Mary died, and the judge and the priest now had no power over Geoffrey; he was a free man and like Bernard Gilpin and all other protestants, he and his wife rejoiced in the deliverance and in hope of better times.

The Queen herself, for whose accession the protestants were rightly so thankful, loved her people and was pleased with their loyalty and joy. But the pope was watching her and there were papists who might claim her throne; she wanted to go warily. She was determined to be supreme head of the church, but she wanted to keep the goodwill of her Romanist subjects, and that was not easy. She and her great men looked over the prayer-book used in the days of King Edward VI, and struck out the passage in the litany about the tyranny of the bishop of Rome, used with such fervour by her protestant subjects. A few other alterations were made, to make the book less protestant. The Queen wanted to let the old priests carry on in the use of the vestments they had been accustomed to wear; whereas to some of the godly protestants, the surplice, the plainest garment of them all, seemed a rag of popery, and they would not wear it; they wished for more, not less, purity in worship, and hence they

were called Puritans. Others, and among them godly men also, wore the surplice, thinking it plain and decent enough; it was not a point of conscience with them. The Queen's wish however was to be law in the matter; her decisions with regard to public worship were embodied in the Act of Uniformity, which was passed by Parliament in June 1559. It was enacted that all in the realm whether protestant or papist should worship in all points according to the book of common prayer. In this lay Geoffrey Hurst's chief trouble.

The Queen's visitors came to Pennington and chose four protestants to see that the people complied with the Act; Geoffrey was one, and a friend of his, Henry Brown, was another. It was not part of the duty of the four men to see that the clergymen complied; men in higher social position than they were saw to that; their part was to see that all the parishioners attended church, and to fine them if they absented themselves without proper excuse. The church

PENNINGTON CHURCH, LANCS.

had been cleansed from crosses and images; Henry Brown
had been one of the first to take them out. A table had been
put in, and the popish altar taken out, and the service and
Scripture reading were all in English instead of Latin. So far
it was a satisfaction to the four men. God has said that His
Word shall not return to Him void, but will prosper in the
thing whereto He sends it. Many careless ungodly people
were now obliged to hear it, and who could tell but that
every Lord's day it might please God to send it into the
hearts of one or many whom He purposed to save? That
time indeed was described afterwards as the time when
throughout the country "God's Word began to prevail."

But in Geoffrey Hurst's town Pennington the minister was
the old priest Parkinson, and the duty of seeing that the
minister carried out the law fell to Thomas Lelond, the
Justice of the Peace—the two who had tried to get rid of
him! The judge went to church as seldom as he could, but
when he went he took with him his dog whose collar was
covered with bells; and during the whole time of the service
he played with the dog, and often the sound of the bells
drowned the voice of Mr. Parkinson—who, indeed, used his
voice as badly as he could. Then the judge would have mass
performed by Parkinson privately in his own house.

Things went on in that way for a long time, these two
men still wishing to revenge themselves on the protestants
for their escape. Neither were they the only two in the little
town who hated the righteous, and at last a malicious neigh-
bour of Henry Brown brought a false charge of theft against
him. The charge was proved untrue, but Judge Lelond ruled
that as Brown would or might or was capable of even picking
a purse, he should be followed up. So, in a great heat he
appointed a day upon which he should go to Lancaster gaol.
Then came one of the long list of "God's judgments upon
persecutors;" before that day the judge fell down dead without a moment's warning.

By that time Geoffrey Hurst had ended his weary pilgrim-
age. He had not long taken up his work of inspection, when
"being sore grieved with the office, he fell sick." Conflicting

thoughts filled his mind; here was the protestant church, but there was no godly man in the pulpit; obedience to the Queen was a duty, yet his office was most distasteful. Searching into the whereabouts of those who were not at church reminded him of being spied upon himself, the year before. He was not strong; hiding about in Yorkshire had undermined his health, and now want of sleep and an illness brought him low. Do what Mrs. Hurst could to 'swage' his pain with 'cataplasms' or soothe his cough with comfortable cordials and possets, she lost her good husband—he died.

However, when Geoffrey knew that his days on earth were numbered he was happy. He had peace and great joy before he fell asleep in Jesus. He died "making a very godly end."

It must have been a mournful time for the little knot of friends in Pennington who had been accustomed to meet at midnight in Geoffrey's house in Queen Mary's reign. Then, although in jeopardy every hour, they had found the word of the Lord precious; the preaching of the four Yorkshire ministers had brought strength and comfort to their souls. But now, after the Act of Uniformity, those ministers could not come. Would Parkinson suffer such men to preach in his pulpit? Never! Why not meet in the house as before and invite them to come on the Lord's day occasionally? Because the law was that everybody must go to church, and three of the little midnight assembly were the men appointed to see that the law was obeyed. Besides, Mr. Reneses and Mr. Best, Mr. Broadbank and Mr. Russell had most probably returned to the charge of their own flocks, amidst a joy like that of the people at Houghton-le-Spring.

In Lancashire, for a very long time there was no godly preacher except in Rochdale. There, one Mr. Hargreaves was Vicar, and after him Mr. Midgley, of whom we will hear more. The Bishop of Chester, in whose diocese Lancashire was, did not further preaching as Dr. Pilkington, Bishop of Durham, did. He was strict in pressing protestants to conformity with every detail of the Act, but with papists he "for friendliness sake did not wish to disturb them." The majority of the people were still Romanists, and it was soon said,

"How few on the Sabbath days are to be found in the churches and yet the ale-houses are full, and here is living the Bishop of Man" (away from his charge in the Isle of Man) "as merrily as Pope Joan."

And so it may be that these early Elizabethans proved, as so many people have done, that their individual times of prosperity or happiness had been in a time of general distress, and their distress in a time of general prosperity. To God's people it is only when He giveth quietness that others cannot make trouble; when He begins to cut *their* Israel short, they *are* cut short. And yet the whole building, though going "round about," goes round about "upward," and all things work together for their good.

Going back now, you remember that Geoffrey Hurst was the brother-in-law of George Marsh, who was martyred in Mary's days. I will just remind you of him, and if you want to read any more, you will find several pages in Foxe's Book of Martyrs. George married when he was twenty-five, and they lived on a farm and God gave them a nice little family. He became a minister, and his sermons and Bible readings did a lot of good in that part of Lancashire. But after Edward VI died, Mary came to the throne, and persecution followed. He was told the authorities were after *him*—what was he to do? Run away? or stay where he was, depending on God's strength to witness a good confession? People of God, faced with such questions, have felt differently. However, after George had met a friend on Dean Moor one day at sunset, and had prayed together, his mind was more settled; he would stay.

And soon the authorities, in league with the Romanist priests, had him in their hands, and examined him; then they put him in a tiny stone prison, cold and windy, with no bed, only a few canvas tent-cloths to lie on, no-one to see him, only the keeper twice a day with food and drink. Later they took him to Chester, and then he was condemned in the Lady Chapel of the cathedral there, and sentenced to be burnt to death. His prison-keeper, finding he should lose him, said with tears, "Farewell, good George." They put him in a dungeon in Northgate until the day appointed, all alone, but some godly people in the evening used to call out to him and ask him how he was, and he would reply to them cheerfully.

The day came, and they led him forth; after he had kneeled to pray, they chained him to the post, having a number of faggots under him, and a barrel with tar in over his head. The fire was lit, and he suffered long; but finally yielded his spirit to the Lord with those words, "Father of heaven, have mercy upon me." He durst not deny his Saviour Christ, lest he lose his mercy everlasting, and so win everlasting death.

This is what he wrote to some friends at Manchester: 'The only way to heaven is through much tribulation. For the kingdom of heaven is like unto a city built and set upon a broad field, and full of all good things; but the entrance thereof is narrow, like as it were a burning flame on one hand and deep water on the other; and as it were one straight path between them, so narrow that one person only can pass at a time. If this city were now given to an heir, and he never went through the perilous way, how could he receive his inheritance? Wherefore, seeing we are in this narrow way which leadeth to the most joyful city of everlasting life, let us not halt or turn back afraid of the danger; but follow Christ and be fearful of nothing, no not even of death itself, for this must lead to our journey's end, and open to us the gate of everlasting life.'

Bold Rothwell

IN the sermons of Mr. Richard Rothwell, a native of Bolton in Lancashire, there was no gospel teaching. He himself thought them wonderful because they had so many Latin and Greek quotations. He "sauced" his sermons, as Archbishop Grindal had said, "with much fineness and exornation of speech," in order to make up in supposed eloquence for one particle of edification.

Mr. Rothwell "was of a very goodly and majestic presence," tall, strong, and fond of bowling, fishing and shooting. Archery was always a great feature in the education of Lancashire boys; Manchester Grammar School had specialised in it from its foundation early in the century, and Mr. Rothwell delighted in his bow and arrow.

In his circle of friends were two knights who were at daggers drawn with each other. Their pastor would fish in the fish-ponds of one and present the fish to the other; and hunt in the park of the other, and enjoy the resultant venison and the joke with his enemy. He was trespassing thus one evening in the park when just as his arrow had brought down a stag the game-keeper appeared and accosted him. Mr. Rothwell was not to be baulked for restraint of a little physical strength. He laid the game-keeper down on the ground, bound him by the thumbs and tied him to a tree letting his feet just touch the ground. Then he went on his way and it was not until the next day that the game-keeper was found and unbound.

One Saturday afternoon he was playing bowls on the green of a friend near Rochdale. The company was composed mostly of Romanists; he numbered many such among his friends. To their surprise, they saw someone coming in to the green—Mr. Midgley, the vicar of Rochdale.

1560	1570	1580	1590	1600	1610	1620	1630	1640
Elizabeth I					JAMES I		Charles I	
		Mr. Midgley						
	RICHARD ROTHWELL							

Mr. Midgley was greatly inferior to Mr. Rothwell in mind, body and possessions, being a poor clergyman of few gifts. But he had great grace. Mr. Rothwell's attitude to him—for he knew him quite well—was one of half-patronising annoyance. Mr. Midgley came straight up to his young fellow-clergyman, and asked him to come and speak to him. They sat down a little way off from the bowling-green. What Mr. Midgley said was to the effect that Mr. Rothwell had many qualities that he had always admired, his talents were far greater than his own, and what a pity it was that he should spend his time with Papists. To be playing bowls on a Saturday afternoon was not what a minister should be doing—he should be preparing for the Sabbath day. Mr. Rothwell snuffed—what interference! "Well . . ." said Mr. Midgley, and went home and prayed.

The game was quite spoilt for Mr. Rothwell; he went home, all his light-heartedness gone. The next day (how he provided for his own congregation is not recorded) he went to hear Mr. Midgley preach. Little had he thought on Saturday morning that the next day, after service in Mr. Midgley's church, he would go and thank him for his sermon and ask him to pray for him. But "thou knowest not what a day may bring forth," and so it was. Conviction of sin deepened in his soul; for a long time he was comfortless, but at last while he was listening to Mr. Midgley on another occasion he had a joyful assurance of the pardon of his sin. It was another *change for the better*.

After his conversion his preaching underwent a great change. Sometimes the people cried out in the church through strong conviction of sin; sometimes they went away filled

with the consolations of the gospel. The epithet—Bold—was
not added to his name till his later years, which were not in
the days of Queen Elizabeth.

Because of his straightforward preaching in exposing all
sham and sin, people called Mr. Rothwell 'the rough hewer',
for he cut them down 'root and branch.' He was so sure of
persecution, he would never marry, often saying, 'Persecution
is the pledge of future happiness.'

For many years he was a 'lecturer' at a chapel in Lancashire, but then removed to Barnard Castle in county Durham.
A good lady told him she was afraid about his going among
such rude and fierce people, so he replied, "Madam, if I
thought I should not meet the devil, I would not go: he and
I have been at odds in other places, and I hope we shall not
agree there." Well, the people received him there, and helped
support him. He seldom preached a sermon which did not
bring some poor wandering sinner to God. Once a person
collected a lot of money for him from his friends, but when
Mr. Rothwell knew of it, he caused it to be returned to the
donors, saying he sought not *theirs* but *them*. Many came a
long way full of fun, to hear him and then find fault and
make sport—but they returned home convinced of their sins,
inquiring what they must do to be saved.

He ended his days at Mansfield, Notts. While he was
poorly, he told his friends, "I shall soon be well. I shall ere
long be with Christ." At the last he asked those round him

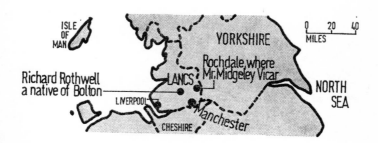

to sing a psalm; and while they were singing his spirit took its flight to sing the song of Moses and the Lamb for ever.

The Mr. Midgley, who had come and spoken to him on the bowling-green all those years ago, was a good man, and laboured at Rochdale nearly fifty years, and God used his ministry in the conversion of thousands of souls. We have a lovely glimpse of him, observing the Lord's Supper, taking the broken bread round to the members in a basket, each person quietly putting in his hand to take a piece out. And after his labours had ended, his son was vicar of Rochdale after him.

The Stately Homes of England

FROM time immemorial every hall and manor in England had had its chaplain. The priest generally exercised a considerable influence in the family, and in the Middle Ages that influence was on the side of Rome, except in the few cases in which the chaplain favoured the doctrines of Wyclif and the Lollards. With the Reformation the manor house chaplains became Protestant. But Sir Robert Cotton, in his 'Lament for the Prophesyings', sorrows that in many of them Protestant ministers had possessed these private chaplaincies for only a little time, and Jesuits were in their places. Numbers of Jesuits had begun to work about four years before. The suppression of the Prophesyings was their great opportunity; turning with the tide was Rome's hope. A new chaplain comes to the old manor house. He makes a point from the beginning, of showing appreciation of the family it is his delight to serve. Pride of ancestry perceptibly increases; and better still, an increased affection twines round the family traditions until in the end nothing suits the 'old family' but the 'old religion'—blatant popery.

In some cases the Jesuit no doubt had little difficulty. In other cases he may have found his task no easy one. The family may have seen the errors of popery quite clearly long before, and been glad that the Queen had made it safe to profess Protestantism. In some cases allegiance had no doubt been divided. Here, in intellectual disputes, the Jesuit would know exactly how much argument or insinuation to throw into each scale to bring the weight down, finally, on the side of Rome. Where Protestantism was not of the heart, but of the head only, he too often succeeded.

In bright contrast are the records of individual members of ancient houses, called by the Holy Spirit of God from the darkness of centuries to the knowledge of His salvation and the proclamation of His Gospel. On such pages of their family history a light from heaven shines: "Arise, shine, for thy light is come, and the glory of the Lord is risen upon thee."

Here are three such records.

The first record is of LAURENCE CHADDERTON. The Chaddertons were a Lancashire family. One, Henry de Chadderton, in 1378 held the important office of bailiff of the Wapentake of West Derby, one of the six Hundreds into which Lancashire was then divided. It is interesting to find "Leverpole" and other towns included in West Derby, seeing that this name survives to-day only as a district in the great port of Liverpool. The family seat was near Oldham, at a place that still bears the name—Chadderton. There Laurence was born in the year 1546. He was sent to London to study law, and it was said he went for the law and was found by the gospel, but by what means, is not I think on record. After having been in the Inns of Court a short time, he found little liking for the legal profession. He felt impelled to go to Cambridge and was admitted to Christ's College as a 'poor scholar' (i.e. a 'sizar', doing menial duties in place of full fees). Not until then did he tell his father of this change. He had been 'much nuzled up in popish superstition' by his father, to whom it was now evident that a great change of mind had come over his son. In reply he sent him a small parcel containing a pocket or 'poke', in which was a groat "to go a-begging withal."

When his father thus forsook him, the Lord brought him even more than before into favour and tender love (Daniel 1) with the Master and Fellows of the College. They saw that he had an indefatigable zeal and he was chosen to be a Fellow while he was still only a Bachelor of Arts. He was one of a group of divinity students who together pored over the Scriptures, searching into the true sense of the Hebrew and Greek text until, as it is said, "They went out like

Apollos, eloquent men and mighty in the Scriptures, and the Lord was with them, so that they brought in a very great harvest into God's barn." Clearly, the Elizabethan divines believed in the *work* of the ministry; they gave themselves wholly to it (1 Tim. 4. 15) and all this, in dependence upon the power of the Holy Spirit, that they might enter into the experience of God's people and minister to the doubting troubled heart.

Chadderton was a great preacher. Early in his career in 1578, he had once been chosen to preach to the crowds of people who flocked round St. Paul's Cross. In 1583, the year of Grindal's death, Sir Walter Mildmay founded Emmanuel College, Cambridge asking Dr. Chadderton to be the master. At first he declined the honour but Sir Walter said that unless he would consent, he would not found the college at all. Emmanuel became very eminently a Puritan 'school of the prophets'. Dr. Chadderton, concerned for the maintenance of pure doctrine after his death, and fearing that when he died an Arminian would be appointed to succeed him, resigned his mastership while he had interest in the succession. (That, however, was not until the year 1622.) His lectures in St. Clements Church in Cambridge were the resort of great numbers of people for sixteen years.

An incident is related about his preaching in another place. Whether his father was dead, or by whatever providence it was, he was at his old home, Chadderton, visiting his friends. They asked him to preach and he did so to a vast audience. Having continued for two hours, he said that he feared he had trespassed on his hearers' time long enough.

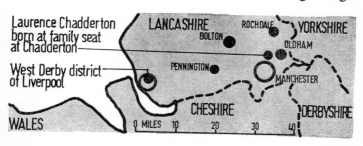

Laurence Chadderton born at family seat at Chadderton

West Derby district of Liverpool

LANCASHIRE
BOLTON
ROCHDALE
YORKSHIRE
OLDHAM
PENNINGTON
MANCHESTER
CHESHIRE
DERBYSHIRE
WALES
0 MILES 10 20 30 40

1540	1550	1560	1570	1580	1590	1600	1610	1620	1630	1640
	E	M	Elizabeth I				James I		Charles I	
Born at Chadderton.		Preached at St. Pauls Cross.		◄ Master of Emmanuel College. ►						

LAURENCE CHADDERTON

With one voice the whole congregation cried out, "Go on, Sir, go on, for God's sake go on, sir, go on, go on!" He went on in the warmth of his subject and to the feasting of their souls, and there was an awakening and great revival. And that was in Lancashire—such a desert in the days of poor Geoffrey Hurst and of Bishop Pilkington. And it is not without significance that Lancashire, even the Hundred of West Derby, has often since that day been foremost in the stand for Protestantism as England's heritage—a heritage of the everlasting Gospel as preached by Dr. Chadderton on that occasion.

He was one of the translators of the Authorised Version, and eventually lived to be 102. He could read to the end without spectacles. During his long married life, no one was ever kept at home from public worship to do the cooking. He used to say, "I desire as much to have my servants to know the Lord as myself."

The second is that of THOMAS GATAKER. The Gataker family had lived in Gataker (or Gatacre) Hall near Bridgenorth in Shropshire from the days of King Edward the Confessor. Thomas, a son of the house in Queen Mary's reign, was studying law in the Temple, like Chadderton. He had access to the examinations of some of the Protestant prisoners. He saw and heard the martyrs, and 'observing their meekness and patience, and with what evidence of truth and resolution of mind they maintained faith and a good conscience, he was led to seek their God and their happiness.'* Thomas *found* the Lord, and *his* parents too perceived a

* Biographica Evangelica

change in him which they did not like. They feared his professing himself a Protestant and so sent him to France, and 'to win him to a compliance with them in religion they settled upon him an estate in a lease of £100 per annum in old rents. But like St. Paul he counted all outward advantages as nothing in comparison with the knowledge of Jesus Christ. His father therefore, perceiving how fixed and unmovable he was in his choice of religion, recalled him to England and in great displeasure revoked his former grant of £100 per annum which yet could not be effected without his son's consent. But this young disciple had already learned the hard lesson of self-denial, and of forsaking all to follow Christ, and therefore to preserve his conscience pure and entire he gave up that which was intended as a bait for apostacy.' His father's anger increased and he threw off Thomas altogether. But now he experienced the blessedness of the words in the twenty-seventh Psalm: "When my father and my mother forsake me, then the Lord will take me up;" and 'the Lord', as Clark's narrative goes on, 'raised him up friends by whose assistance and encouragement he pursued his studies in Oxford, and in process of time, when not only the clouds of ignorance and superstition were dispelled but also those bloody storms in the Marian days were blown over, he took upon him the public ministry of the gospel.'

Mr. Gataker first exercised his ministry as private chaplain to the Earl of Leicester, but shortly afterwards was appointed to the living of St. Edmund's, Lombard Street, where he preached at the very time Archbishop Grindal was weeping

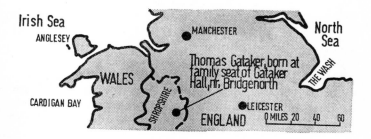

Irish Sea · ANGLESEY · MANCHESTER · North Sea · WALES · Thomas Gataker, born at family seat of Gataker Hall, nr. Bridgenorth · THE WASH · CARDIGAN BAY · SHROPSHIRE · LEICESTER · ENGLAND · 0 MILES 20 40 60

1540	1550	1560	1570	1580	1590	1600	1610	1620	1630	1640
	E	M	Elizabeth I				James I		Charles I	
The martyrs ■ ◄ London preacher ►										
Thomas Gataker										
				Thomas Gataker, junior						►

himself blind at the thought that preaching was to be allowed no longer. Here he continued to preach the Word of life until his death in 1593. He left behind him a son of his own name, who became famous in the congregation, and died in the time of the Commonwealth, after having been in the ministry at Rotherhithe most of his days.

The third record is of ARTHUR HILDERSHAM. Arthur's father belonged to an 'antient' family at Stetchworth in Cambridgeshire. His mother's family was not ancient only, but among the great ones of the earth, being a branch of the royal House of York and of Warwick the King-maker, and she was cousin to Henry the Earl of Huntingdon. She had not departed from the Church of Rome, and her husband though less zealous was also an unenlightened Romanist. Her brother Sir Arthur Pole was pining in the Tower of London as a prisoner. He had plotted in favour of Mary Queen of Scots, and in an attempt to restore royal honour and freshness to the faded White Rose. His sister's little son, born in 1563, was named after him. While in the Tower he carved on the wall a device with the motto; A passage perillus makethe a port pleasant. How unlike his perils were those to which his little nephew was born—the rough and stormy seas of the Court of High Commission, through which he sailed oftener than almost any man, before the Sabbath evening in 1632 when he entered his pleasant heavenly port.

When Arthur was a little boy and already having been taught to repeat his prayers in Latin, Mr. Hildersham sent him to a school in Saffron Walden because many gentlemen's sons went there. Now it happened that Mr. Desborough the master was a Protestant, and not only did he teach Arthur scripturally from the Bible, but had the joy of seeing real marks of grace in him. It was the same at Cambridge; his tutor there, a man who loved him for his grace, was one of the last Mr. Hildersham would have chosen for his son if he had been at all on the alert. But when Arthur was fifteen, his father, waking up to it all, determined that the best way to eradicate the unthought-of heresy, was to send him to Rome. His great-uncle, Cardinal Pole, had lived in Rome for a long time, and Mr. Hildersham knew that friends would soon provide him with a tempting post.

But he would not go to Rome and his father, vexed with his son, thought of the expedient of the Ordinaries. The Ordinaries were the forerunners of the London clubs, and those that Mr. Hildersham patronised were frequented by none but Romanists—well-born cultured Romanists, ready to speak on any topic, and some of them charming and persuasive. Card-playing always followed the Club meal, and most of the Ordinaries were hunting-grounds for the disguised sharpers who abounded in the city. Mr. Hildersham however may have had no idea of this. But while day after day passed, father and son meeting all the "best catholics" Mr. Hildersham could think of, Arthur seemed no more inclined than he was at the first to get into the spirit of the Ordinary. He only saw, knew and felt, that it was all wicked and he was preserved from being charmed by anyone. His father's hatred rose and as he could not turn him into the

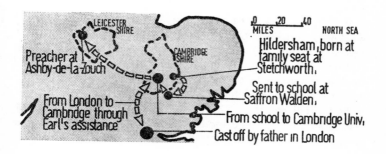

Preacher at Ashby-de-la-Zouch

From London to Cambridge through Earl's assistance

LEICESTERSHIRE

CAMBRIDGESHIRE

0 20 40
MILES   NORTH SEA

Hildersham, born at family seat at Stetchworth.

Sent to school at Saffron Walden.

From school to Cambridge Univ.

Cast off by father in London

Church of Rome he turned him adrift, his son of fifteen, to wander "run aground with poverty" as Fuller says, in the streets of London alone.

I will give Samuel Clark's account of his deliverance. He says: "Being in this dejected and forlorn condition, God who comforteth them that are cast down, comforted him by meeting with Master John Ireton (then Fellow of Christ's College, after Rector of Kegworth in Leicestershire, a man famous for piety and learning). Who, at their meeting said unto him, 'Arthur, why art thou so long from thy book, and losest so much time?' 'Alas! Sir,' said he, 'I shall go no more to Cambridge,' and thereupon told him his condition and what had caused it. 'Be not discouraged,' saith Master Ireton, 'thou hast a noble kinsman whom I will acquaint with thy case, and I doubt not but he will provide for thee.' Accordingly Master Ireton soon after went to the Right Honourable Henry Earl of Huntingdon, Lord President of the North (whose mother and Master Hildersham's mother were cousins) and told him the sad condition of his poor kinsman. The noble earl gladly embraced this opportunity of doing good and sent for him, encouraged him, promised him maintenance, and gave orders to Master Ireton to send him back to Cambridge and to place him with a good tutor, 'for,' said he, 'I suppose his father placed him with a papist.' But when Master Ireton assured him of the contrary, he gave orders he should go to his former tutor, of whose love to him and care of him Master Hildersham was wont often to speak." So the Lord superintended all these changes for the better.

We are told that Mr. Hildersham began his ministry in weakness and fear, but at his first sermon, seeing a friend before him who he thought was praying for him, he took courage and was not confounded. In 1587 the Earl of Huntingdon appointed him to be preacher at Ashby-de-la-Zouch, where his castle was, but not until 1593 did he appoint him to be vicar there; the two offices were often separate. He had been silenced for some months in 1590, and from that time onward it was evident that the Court of High Commission was particularly galled that one of such high birth should be found amongst the Puritans. The Queen's reign however was not the time they followed him up with malicious intent; several times danger threatened "but God in mercy prevented it."

ASHBY de la ZOUCH CHURCH, LEICS.

An instance of this kind occurred in 1596. The Assizes were being held in Leicester. The judge, Judge Anderson, was an implacable High Churchman.

It was a time of dearth and general distress, and the preacher was looked to to answer the question: "Why has this distress befallen us?" Mr. Hildersham read out his text: "And it came to pass, when Ahab saw Elijah, that Ahab said unto him, Art thou he that troubleth Israel? and he answered, I have not troubled Israel, but thou and thy father's house, in that ye have forsaken the commandments of the Lord, and thou hast followed Baalim" (1 Kings 18. 17, 18). As he preached the judge grew furious, got up, and was going out of the church, when Mr. Hildersham addressed him with such authority that he sat down again. He did not however forgive the preacher, but tried to induce the grand

1550	1560	1570	1580	1590	1600	1610	1620	1630

E M | Elizabeth I | | | James I

◄ Earl of Huntingdon

Cast off by his father ►█◄ Preacher at Ashby-de-la-Zouch ►

ARTHUR HILDERSHAM

jury to indict him, "but it would have been hard," says his biographer, "to have found a grand jury in Leicestershire that would have done that."

During one period of his ministry he lectured every Tuesday for nearly two years on John chapter 4; and at a later time he gave 152 lectures on Psalm 51.

Soon after he was appointed 'preacher' at Ashby, Mr. Hildersham married a young lady named Ann Barfoot from Lambourn Hall in Essex: and they had seven little children at Ashby.

During one of these 'silent' times, he was sheltering at a house in Hampstead when he became very ill, and nearly died. But those who were nursing him heard him say inside his bed-curtains (I suppose he was in a 'four-poster') the words of Psalm 118.17, "I shall not die, but live, and declare the works of the LORD." In 1628 the Lectures on John 4 were printed in a book, and the next February Mr. Hildersham had a letter from his friend John Cotton. John had had a letter from a Dutch minister in London who had sent some of these books to several ministers abroad, and please could they have the Lectures on Psalm 51 printed too. And eventually these too appeared in a book.

He had interruptions to his ministry caused by enemies, once being fined £2000 (in *those* days!) for not exactly observing every detail of ceremony in the Church of England services. Referring to those intervals when he was not allowed to preach, he said "If it please the Lord to let His ministers suffer so, it is either because their testimony is finished, or because God will receive more honour by their suffering and constant confession of his truth, than by their peace." While he was in hiding more or less, a sleuth was sent by the Bishop of London who broke into his study at Ashby, and took away many valuable books.

ARTHUR HILDERSHAM

Sometimes he was able to listen to other ministers, and he used to say he never heard any faithful preacher of the gospel however mean his talents might be, but he could discover some gift in him that was wanting in himself, and could receive some profit from his preaching. What an example for us all!

After he died, I think it must have been someone who loved his ministry who wrote in the Ashby burial register this entry: 'March 6: Mr. Arthur Hildersam, minister of Ashby, a worthy and faithful servant of God—a famous Divine and a painful (painstaking) preacher, the comfort of God's people in his time, departed this life the 4th of March, and was interred in the chancel of our parish church in Ashby the sixth.' And a tablet to his memory has been placed on the wall, which you can see if you visit Ashby church today—and the Castle ruins too, where the good Earl of Huntingdon lived.

About the time he died, Mr. Hildersham's copy of Minshen's Dictionary was given for the use of the boys at Ashby School, and a Mr. William Cox was paid a shilling for putting a 'superscription' on it (remember Matthew 22.20?)—I suppose this was the school crest. Good books deserve to be thought about and looked after, even when their godly owners die—not like those books in Acts 19.19 that were only fit for the bonfire, and the sooner you burn bad books the better.

Now the house where Mr. Hildersham had lived belonged to the School (he had headed the list of feoffees, or trustees), and the rent was ten shillings a year; it had a gate into 'the near commons'; and the house was taken down in 1643. And do you remember all those lectures on Psalm 51, published by his son soon after his death—well, in 1672 they were even translated into Hungarian, so you can tell they went far and wide doing good.

Still later, the Hastings family, who by now had built Ashby Place, a large house on the site of the present manor-house, resided here again; and this was the home of Selina, the Countess of Huntingdon who was so prominent in the Evangelical revival of the eighteenth century. But that is a story for another time.

The Noble House of Huntingdon

1. The President of the North.

A PRAYER of Dr. Pilkington, Bishop of Durham, was: "Lord God . . . raise up, we pray Thee, in these our latter days such faithful servants about the Prince in the Court as Nehemiah was, that would pity the miserable state of the poor people and afflicted church, rather than seek their own ease, wealth and profit." One such in the court of Elizabeth was Henry third Earl of Huntingdon.

When the Queen's captured cousin, Mary Queen of Scots was in England, the Earl was entrusted with the oversight of her for a little while, Elizabeth knowing that he was wise and loyal to herself, and that popish plots on behalf of the Scottish Queen would not escape his vigilance. On the outbreak of a popish rebellion in the North in 1569 the rebels crowded into Durham Cathedral, said Mass and tore the Bible to pieces. The insurgents were joined by such numbers that after all was over, there were "few innocente to trie the giltie." When the leaders of the revolt found that the rest of England did not join them, their scheme failed and they met with unsparing severity. Sir George Bowes, Governor of Barnard Castle, was so severe that Bernard Gilpin pleaded with him for more gentleness; for many of those whom he put to death, "hanging them up by scoars," were mere country people, who seeing a band of armed men had caught up the first farm implement they saw and joined them. A Council was established at York, for the rule of that "cuntre in so grete miserie;" and the Earl of Huntingdon was made President of it. As such he neither sought nor found wealth or profit, and ease he found only when he returned to his old castle at Ashby-de-la-Zouch, and there had such sweet gratification as rescuing his young cousin Arthur Hildersham from popery and want.

The Earl's Northern castle, Sheriff Hutton near York, was not far from the border of the "Debateable Land" of Bernard Gilpin. He may have met Gilpin—the Apostle of the North; let us hope that he did; let us hope that he met Bishop Pilkington for they were like-minded. But Pilkington died in 1575 and was succeeded by Dr. Barnes, a prelate of another type. The great task of the Council, and therefore particularly of the Earl of Huntingdon, was not so much to bring cattle-drivers to justice (six hundred "kie" driven out of Tyndale was easy to deal with)—but to make it impossible for another popish rising to succeed. One preventive was universal in the country—fining and imprisoning those who absented themselves from church. Most probably the Earl enforced that law upon popish recusants without two thoughts, and Bishop Barnes and the Archbishop of York would uphold him, high churchmen in those days having a due abhorrence of popery, especially in the treachery of its political aspect. And so, as far as that was his work, the Earl satisfied the Queen, but he was well aware that his position was insecure. He incurred the dislike of Bishop Barnes and the Archbishop of York because he stood by William Whittingham the Dean of Durham, whom they disliked. To explain this dislike we must look back some years.

In King Edward's reign Whittingham was famous in Oxford for his great learning, and in Queen Mary's reign he had

1530	1540	1550	1560	1570	1580	1590	1600	1610
Henry VIII		E	M		Elizabeth I			James I
Mary Stewart flees Scotland ■ ▶ Northern popish rebellion ■ ■ ▶				◀ President of the North ▶				
3rd Earl of Huntingdon								

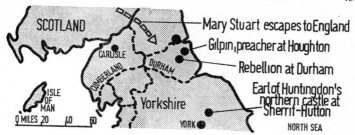

been an exile in Geneva. Much of the Bible known as the Geneva Bible had been of his translation and together with Sternhold and Hopkins he had transposed many of the psalms into metre. Both Knox and Calvin had been his close friends. He had been ordained at Geneva while the permanent form of the English service was still under discussion. The controversies were sadly full of bitterness, but when Whittingham returned from exile he was made Dean of Durham through the influence of his warm friend Bishop Pilkington, and exercised his "learned, godly, and painful ministry" in happy unity with the Bishop. But now, because his ordination had been of a more Presbyterian form than the State recognised, his case was under discussion for trial as contrary to the Act of Uniformity. Bishop Barnes could not endure him, and the Archbishop of York wanted to deny his ordination. The Earl presided in the Court and refused to deprive him, saying that all the godly at home and abroad would take it very ill if ministers duly ordained in a reformed church were disallowed, and popish priests ignorant and godless were allowed, only because their ordination was episcopal.

His ruling may have been a cause of displeasure to the Queen. We find Sir Francis Walsingham writing soon after about a "new mislike" the Queen entertained towards him. Her Majesty was not at home with the Earl as she was with the courtiers who flattered her. Four times she said that she would honour his castle at Ashby-de-la-Zouch with a visit but four times she hesitated. The Earl and Countess made preparations but each time the Queen cancelled the arrangement. Lord Hunsden the Queen's cousin, was his enemy; he disliked the Earl's religion, and belittled his ability to rule, and he was one who more than most men might say what he liked to the Queen. Like Daniel and Nehemiah, the Earl carried on his duties, letting his eyes look right on, through "thwarts" and "mislikes" till the Autumn of 1595. Plague ravaged the Northern towns that year. It was perhaps the cause of his death. He died in the midst of his work, sending a despatch one day to London and being ill for only two days immediately after. His death was a great grief to his devoted brother, Sir Francis Hastings. "Good Sir Francis," wrote the Earl of Pembroke, "I request you not to take your brother's death to heart more than Christianity and wisdom should." But Sir Francis could not help mourning, and the bereaved Countess of Huntingdon "continuing in such sorrow and heaviness as greater could not be in any creature living," soon followed her husband to the grave. Sheriff Hutton—the ancient castle of George, Duke of Clarence—was sold, and "the servauntes in thousolde of the Rt. Hon. Hy. Earl of Hunt.:" were scattered—the gentlemen, the yeomen, the cooks, the serving-men, "the wood-herde, the slaughter-man and the children of the kitchen." An inventory was made; the Earl had died without "wealth and profit," and each room, small as well as great, was valued. Amongst the small were the following:—

"One bedstead, one truckle bedstead, one great book of mappes, one great Tremellius Bible, the latter in two books—to be £4 11 8."

"In the chamber beyonde the kitchinge where Mr. Gilbye doth lye—Total 46/6."

"In the men's chamber next thereto 15/4."

"In the chamber where the kitchinge boyes do lie—10/-."

"In the chamber next to the church where Mr. Barricho doth lye—one liverye."

"In the lowe gallerye at the old house—one globe of the world, one mappe of Europe, one mappe of Spain, one mappe of the Low Countries, one mappe of Scotland, one table in a frame containinge the causes of salvacion and damnacion."

"Item, In my Lord's little chamber next the gallerye and in my Lo:'s bedchamber, one table of the ten commandments."

2. Ashby-de-la-Zouch

In the Spring of 1596, the mortal remains of the Earl of Huntingdon were brought to Ashby-de-la-Zouch and interred with great pomp and great sorrow. The Earl had been "good lord" to all in the Castle and in the little town. There he often met Sir Francis and Sir Edward Hastings, the two out of his eight brothers who upheld and followed him in every good work. They came and went. But there was one man of special interest and importance who, going to the Castle at the beginning of the Queen's reign, remained there till his death more than twenty years later, and that was Anthony Gilby, Chaplain to the family and Vicar of the parish. It was not his chamber but his son's, that was "beyond the kitchinge" in the northern Castle. Ashby was his home and he was said to rule there like a bishop. Now there were few of the bishops *in office* of whom Mr. Gilby approved. Like William Whittingham he was "a stickler for the Geneva discipline," i.e., he was a Presbyterian and opposed to the rule of the Church by bishops. He and Whittingham had been together in exile. John Foxe had lived in his house at Frankfort during one period of his laborious poverty with the records of the martyrdoms, and altogether they had been amongst those exiles who then wished the Reformation to go further, as far indeed as it went under Calvin and Knox. Every writer about the disputes on these subjects depicts the very sad quarrels known as "the troubles of Frankfort." The whisperer and his agents separated chief friends just as he did when Bonner and Gardiner (in the days of King Edward) intercepted a letter written by Calvin to Cranmer and other of his English friends. A correspondence had been passing between them with the utmost friendliness, about the

1510	1520	1530	1540	1550	1560	1570	1580	1590
	HENRY VIII			E M	ELIZABETH I			
	Henry 3rd. Earl of Huntingdon							
		exile with John Foxe ◀ Vicar at Ashby ▶						
	ANTHONY GILBY							

form of the Liturgy—should Protestants in England and Europe have the same form? etc. As Toplady puts it: "Bonner and Gardiner forged a surly, snappish answer to Calvin in the names of the divines to whom his letter had been addressed, but whose hands it had never reached. Calvin being disgusted at the rudeness with which he supposed his overtures had been received, here dropt all thoughts of making any further advances on the subject." This stroke of the enemy had not yet come to light during the time of the exile while the brethren bit and devoured one another. We have known for generations that numbers of God's servants have been used by Him under each form of church government: Episcopal, Presbyterian, Independent and Baptist. But in the days of Queen Elizabeth nearly all men still thought that one form only could have God's blessing, and hence they were not prepared to tolerate a form they disapproved.

But more weighty matters occupied the chaplain's mind. He wrote a treatise on Predestination, and commentaries on the Book of Psalms and the Prophecy of Micah; and he was a pastor, a shepherd to his people.

Ashby was a little place; there were about seventy families besides the Castle family. A little way out was Bristow Park, where John Hall, the Bailiff of Ashby (under the Earl) lived with his large family. Mrs. Hall, a delicate lady, was often tormented by the adversary of souls. Mr. Gilby found her sad one day; it was usually so, but she told him that she felt further from comfort than ever because of a dream from which she awaked that morning—a dream of deliverance, and the thought that it was only a dream added to her despair. She had dreamt that in one of her worst attacks a grave physician took her hand kindly, and assured her it was the last she would ever have. In the dream, her joy at the news was unspeakable, but it was only a dream. Mr. Gilby stayed with her, pressing her not to have any doubts as to the special nature of the dream. On ordinary occasions we must not build on them—"we have a more sure word of prophecy," but he assured her, without any wavering, the dream would prove true. He left her wonderfully cheered, and from that time she had no more of the tormenting onslaughts. God gave that change for the better.

The Ashby group had another friend over at Cambridge! the Earl, his brother (Sir Francis Hastings), and Mr. Gilby were in complete sympathy with THOMAS CARTWRIGHT, who had lost a professorship and been expelled from the University there because he taught Presbyterianism in his lectures on the Acts of the Apostles. The stir this occasioned was so great that when he preached "the sextone was fain to take down the windows by reason of the multitudes that came to hear him."

Dr. Whitgift censured him, but he gained the praise and admiration of the King of Scotland, and the friendship of not a few of the nobility. Young Arthur Hildersham, going between Ashby Castle and Cambridge, became his disciple and life-long friend. They had no sympathy with those who left the National Church and none for the Martin Marprelate Tracts, whose "vein of writing," Sir Francis said, "seemed

Ashby-de-la-Zouch
Earl's castle
Anthony Gilby, chaplain
John Hall, governor

Hildersham
hearer of Cartwright

LEICESTER

John Dod, vicar of Hanwell

OXFORDSHIRE

RIVER SEVERN

LONDON

0 20 40
MILES

North Sea

Thomas Cartwright
preacher in Cambridge

THOMAS CARTWRIGHT

little to savour of a well-seasoned spirit." But they thought it equally sinful to comply with "the dregs and rags of popery," and above all they were spiritually-minded men.

In Sir Francis Hastings' leisure hours he wrote a 'Christian Treatise'. "Yt cannot be hydden," he wrote, "but bursteth out. The spirit indeed cannot be lost, but it may be hydden, not only from other men, but even from the partie hymself that hath yt, as it were a sparke under many cold ashes." Cartwright read the treatise, and "found matter of thanks-

1540	1550	1560	1570	1580	1590	1600	1610	1620
Henry VIII E M		Elizabeth I				James I		
THOMAS CARTWRIGHT								
		Arthur Hildersham						
	John Dod, the deprived Vicar of Hanwell							

giving unto the Lord for Sir Francis's sound knowledge of our holy religion."

Cartwright used to get up every morning at 3 o'clock, after only five hours' sleep, and in later life because of infirmity, did most of his study on his knees. He lived to the end of the Queen's reign and a few months longer, continuing his ministry in the church of Warwick Hospital to within two days of his death and for some time also preached at both of the town churches on the Lord's Day, and one of them on the Saturday too. His last sermon was from Ecclesiastes 12.7, which you can look up. On his deathbed he was occupied with nothing less than "the wonderful and un-utterable joy and comfort that he found, God giving him a glimpse of heaven before he came into it." Some of his affairs he left to Mr. Hildersham, and his funeral sermon was preached by one of Mr. Hildersham's closest friends, Mr. Dod, the deprived Vicar of Hanwell.

3. School and College

In 1567 a Free School was founded at Ashby-de-la-Zouch by the Earl of Huntingdon, and, about the time when Mr. Hildersham was appointed Preacher there, in 1587, the schoolmaster was Mr. George Ainsworth. Mr. Ainsworth was not like many of the 16th century schoolmasters, barbarous wielders of the rod; his aim was to teach the boys in the fear of God and to impart some of his vast learning to those who loved learning.

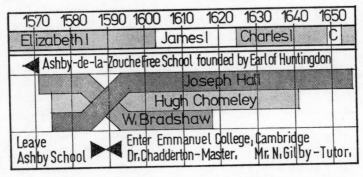

In 1589 three interesting boys left his school in Ashby: William Bradshaw, Hugh Chomeley and Joseph Hall.

Mr. Ainsworth once took a journey to Bosworth, where lived his friend, Nicholas Bradshaw, a gentleman, but very poor. There he found William, aged sixteen or seventeen, just home from school in Worcester, and now having to be put to a manual trade, and very sad on that account. He persuaded his father to let him go to Ashby School, and so interested Mr. Hildersham and Sir Francis Hastings that William went on from school to Emmanuel College. There Mr. Nathaniel Gilby, the son of the old chaplain (who died in 1583) was his tutor.

In later life William Bradshaw looked back with great gratitude and wonder at God's goodness to him. He became a minister, was a peculiarly humble man, amazed that the ministry of one "so vile" was made efficacious to souls; a very contented man, counting himself "passing rich with"— not "forty," but *twenty* "pounds a year" on which to bring up his family. He had an ardent love for Mr. Hildersham, and his children were familiar with the story of how God "stirred up the spirit" of Mr. Ainsworth on the historic visit to their grandfather's house.

Joseph Hall was three years younger than Bradshaw, but was ready to leave school the same term. Though so young, he might quite well be admitted to college; many were admitted younger in those days, and his "parts" were great in his schoolmaster's eyes. He was one of the youngest of the twelve children of that good Mrs. Hall whose God-sent dream and Mr. Gilby's visit were the turning-point in her mental agony.

Joseph's father felt that he could scarcely afford to send him to the University, yet did not want to disregard his son's natural bent. Mr. Ainsworth thought he could solve the problem. He had a great friend in Mr. Pelset, the "lecturer" in Leicester. The Earl had founded a "lecture," and given the lectureship to Mr. Pelset, to preach twice a week, very early in the morning. He had much leisure time, and Mr. Ainsworth thought he would be an excellent tutor for Joseph Hall. So he arranged a meeting between him and Mr. Hall.

Downstairs the elders decided upon the course, and the talk finished with an indenture being drawn up, giving Joseph into Mr. Pelset's care and tuition for seven years. They could not see into the future, but Joseph would be twenty-two years old then, the same age as many graduates, and Mr. Pelset was sure he could equip him for whatever might open to him after that, as well as any tutor in Oxford or Cambridge.

Upstairs was the dear boy—on his knees—committing his way to God. Hugh Chomeley, his lifelong friend and companion, was going to Emmanuel College, but whatever his own lot was to be, he felt peculiarly conscious that it was in God's hands. He never forgot the day in his whole life, and never, he said, more clearly rolled himself upon God's providence.

Joseph was afterwards to be Bishop Hall, whose praise has been in the Church of God ever since, and *this* was the time

> "When first before the mercy-seat,
> He did his all to God commit.
> Who gave him warrant from that hour
> To trust His wisdom, love and power."

That night Joseph went to bed not only with his father's hand in blessing on his head (as was the custom) but with a sense of peace as to his way upon earth. Mr. Pelset went home promising that at a certain time he would send to have the

1570	1580	1590	1600	1610	1620	1630	1640	1650
Elizabeth I				James I		Charles I		C
Earl of Huntingdon		Hall made a Fellow				A Bishop		
		JOSEPH HALL				■■■■■■		
	Nathaniel Gilby							

indenture committed to him, and Mr. Hall promised to send Joseph back with the messenger.

Some time afterwards Joseph's elder brother was one day in Cambridge and saw their family friend Mr. Nathaniel Gilby, who asked him how Joseph was getting on. Hearing all about it he "importunately dissuaded from that course," wishing that if it were at all possible Joseph might be sent to him. When his brother reached home he did not merely tell his father all that had passed, but fell down on his knees before him, and begged that a part of the land which he was to inherit as the elder son, might be sold rather than that Joseph should not go to College. And their father "vehemently assured" his interceding son that Joseph should go whatever it might cost. That moment there was a knock at the door; it was Mr. Pelset's man; he had come to stay all night and to return in the morning with the indentures, and with Joseph. However, he had to go back to Leicester alone, to the wonder, joy and gratitude of Joseph. And so he went to Emmanuel College with his two school-fellows, and Mr. Nathaniel Gilby was their tutor. Joseph looked upon it as a change for the better.

By 1595 the unusual gifts of Joseph Hall seemed to indicate a Fellowship for him at Emmanuel. But as Mr. Gilby was a Fellow, and college rules allowed only one from a county, he prepared to leave Cambridge. Just at that time Hugh Chomeley's father, who like Mr. Hall was under the Earl of Huntingdon in some capacity, had to go to him to York. The Earl enquired how Hugh's friend Joseph Hall was getting on and what were his prospects. For the sake of his excellent father as well as his own, he hoped he was doing well. Mr. Chomeley spoke very highly of his abilities, but when he told the Earl that he was just about to leave Cambridge, the Earl asked, "not without vehemence," why a Fellowship was not given to him. When he heard the reason, he appointed Mr. Gilby chaplain at Sheriff Hutton, promising to compensate him for the loss of his Fellowship. Joseph remained as Fellow of Emmanuel College for six or seven years.

This was the last act of kind patronage that the Earl did for Ashby-de-la-Zouch. He died before the better provisions for the new chaplain at Sheriff Hutton were made, and "the chamber where Mr. Gilbie doth lye" was occupied by him only a little time. Joseph Hall begged that Mr. Gilby might be reinstated, but the rule forbad that, and Dr. Chadderton said that he would have to wait upon the providence of God for his disposing elsewhere. It was probably "a frowning providence" to Mr. Gilby, but unless he was singularly different from his father and whole circle, he would not attribute it to chance. And to Joseph Hall it was a step that led in the end to his becoming a bishop—one of the best bishops of the seventeenth century.

Not far away in Leicester they were also very sorry at the passing of the Earl. There in St. Martin's church he had set up his own pew so that he could hear the 'lecturer' preach there on Wednesday and Friday mornings from 7 a.m. till 8 a.m. Then every year he sent coal for the poor people of Leicester. And he it was who encouraged the Mayor and

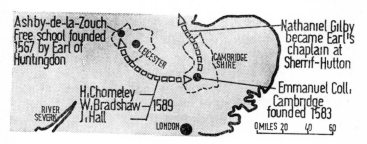

THE OLD LIBRARY, THE GUILDHALL, LEICESTER

Aldermen of Leicester in 1572 to send money through the French church in London to help the French Protestant refugees. And then he thought about the boys in Leicester, and founded a school for them which still stands in High-cross Street; though I don't know what he would have said if he had lived to see four shillings and three pence paid to the town's watchman for watching the grammar school when the naughty boys shut out their Master in 1618.

Then the Earl gave a lot of good books for people to read; they were kept in the belfry at St. Martin's first of all, and then they were moved to the Guildhall, where they are still to be seen today.

Yes, there was much sadness when the good Earl died; but the work of God went on.

Now you remember I told you of Arthur Hildersham, whom the Earl made vicar of Ashby: well, I thought you would like to know that when he was twenty, he wrote to Thomas Cartwright to ask what books he should study, to be a minister; and this is part of the reply:

'The scripture itself shall keep its preeminence still; see that the study of no other writer, however fruitful, shut out some daily reading or meditation therein; for wherever you go out of the paradise of the Holy Scriptures, you shall in the best grounds meet with thorns and thistles, of which you are in danger of pricking if you carry not the forest bill of the Lord's Word wherewith to stub them and crab them up.

It may be doubted whether the Old or New Testament is principally to be laboured in: I think that an equal study of them both is commended unto us; therefore it is not amiss to carry ourselves toward them alike, like two breasts both with milk, so they may be also drawn alike, course by course and one after another. I would esteem that there are some books which require oftener and more diligent study and attentive reading with special attendance—that either their more necessary or general use, or else their difficulty may justly procure them. Among the first are the five books of Moses, and especially the Book of Deuteronomy, the fountain of the rest of the scripture, and wherewith all the prophets after Moses unto the last apostles themselves watered their garden; the book of Joshua also, which even in that part of it which seems to be of least fruit, is of great fruit as that which is the topography almost of the whole Bible . . .

There is some further degree of pains to be taken with some books, among which I count the book of Psalms, the Proverbs and the Epistle to the Romans. And although it be long before a man can fall into any familiar acquaintance with them, yet they are not like the proud and coy dames that despise their suitors, but as those that being written in the spirit of humbleness be open to them that seek to them in the same spirit: and although they speak sometimes as it were but half a word, yet being much about them and often accustomed to talk with them, we shall be like the handmaids which give their continued attendance upon their mistress, even by a beck understand their meaning. But if the time seem longer ere they take us into their privy chamber, the fruit of their nearer acquaintance is so rich as will easily recompence all our travail and attendance.

In the writers which have digged to uncover this treasure to us, yet when you remember the depth and the height on the one side, and the shortness and shallowness of men's wits on the other; when you remember that the foot of no living thing hath trodden upon it, nor any bird (soar it never so high, have it never so quick an eye) hath seen it; it will not be needful to put you in remembrance of the saying of our Saviour Christ, that you take no man to be your father or rabbi here upon earth, nor that you bind your judgment to these things as it were an apprentice to any man, nor to suffer your ear to be nailed to the door of any private man's interpretation, considering that that privilege belongs only to the holy men of God, which spake and wrote by the Holy Spirit of God, and whom God had chosen to be his public notaries, and Recorders of his good pleasure toward us, whom he did sit by, and as it were continually hold their hands while they were writing.'

Foxe's Book of Martyrs

BACK now in 1563, Foxe published the first English edition of his Book of Martyrs. No one thing turned the heart of the English people as a whole from Popery to Protestantism as much as that book. After eight years he published another edition, much longer and fuller. It appeared at such an opportune time that Convocation ordered that it should be placed not only in churches to be read by all comers, but in the colleges at Oxford and Cambridge, and in the halls of private mansions.

This was the answer given to the pope, who had just issued a bull purporting to release Queen Elizabeth's subjects from allegiance to her. But no thunders of Rome or subtle alluring pleas for "the old religion" could command the obedience of *all* who had hitherto been careless. Hundreds reading the accounts of the martyrs in Foxe's book now saw for the first time that "the old religion" was the religion of Babylon, drunk with the blood of the martyrs of Jesus, and they turned to hate it.

Dr. Harpsfield who had consented to the death of many of the martyrs, was furious with Foxe, and under the pseudonym of Alan Cope tried, but in vain, to throw discredit on the book. It can be regarded as nothing less than the work of God to have *given* the book which, in the days of no newspapers, and when the pope was thinking that England might really return to his fold, had such tremendous effect throughout the land.

Years before, on a wild stormy day in 1554 Gardiner the persecutor sent a spy to find and arrest a "heretic" who he suspected was in Ipswich, ready to embark for the Continent. The boat had just gone and the spy returned to London. It was driven back however and the heretic landed again in

1520	1530	1540	1550	1560	1570	1580	1590	1600

Henry VIII   E   M   Elizabeth I

John Foxe

Book of Martyrs ▶

suggestion to write by Lady Jane Grey ▶   exile   ◀ first edition ◀ last edition

Ipswich. To be driven back by storm was such a common occurrence that it was a wonder the spy had not waited at least one day to make sure his victim had escaped him. The boat sailed again the following night and the heretic—John Foxe—was conveyed to safety. He had a manuscript with him—the first part of his book, the history of the martyrs from the time of Wycliffe to 1500, written in Latin. Six or seven years before Lady Jane Grey had proposed to him to write it. He had been a tutor and a preacher in Reigate, but for at least a year his tutorship had ended, and he was left with ample leisure for research and writing. Writing was his element and what he had begun to do was already known. As an exile he lived first at Frankfort and then at Basle. He did manual work for a printer there, earned less than enough for board and lodging for himself, wife and child, but printed his Latin manuscript and sent it abroad, and the learned in every country read it.

That was the first part of the book's history. The author's taste for writing had found its field, ample leisure had been granted, and both writer and writing had been saved by a hairbreadth from destruction. And now God still furthered the work by His providence. Grindal, who had been chaplain to King Edward VI, was an exile also. The thought of a chronicle of current martyrdoms was ever present with him; he was always receiving accounts from friends in England. One great friend was Archdeacon Philpot, that one of the noble army who exclaimed, "I will pay my vows in thee, O Smithfield!" He collected from his imprisoned brethren records of long disputes held with them by their judges the priests. There was a distinct determination in the martyrs to write these records; their spirits were stirred up to the work.

Long accounts of examinations were sent by Philpot to Grindal, and Grindal passed them on to Foxe. And simple pathetic accounts reached him from other places, for the

JOHN FOXE

vows of the martyrs were not all paid in Smithfield—Oxford, Canterbury, Lewes, Colchester, Coventry, villages, towns, and cities, all had their story to tell. Though Foxe heard many of these from the lips of eye-witnesses in the days of peace afterwards, there was a small, sad, but constant stream of them coming to him at Frankfort, at Strasburg and at Basle. And who knows how many risks and preservations that meant? Surely they met them at every turn, for the jail keepers were not all kind and gentle; servants were not all above confessing to the priests that their masters *wrote* they knew not what; and people on outward bound ships were searched for papers. To each of the prominent leaders of the exiles these papers and letters brought news of some chariot of fire and its occupier.

Foxe himself would receive such from Coventry. How many of the readers of his book have loved the stories of the Coventry martyrs!—the story of Laurence Saunders, who died saying, "Welcome the cross of Christ! Welcome everlasting life!", the story of Robert Glover, whose soul was cast down in prison through fear that he would never see Him with joy whom his soul loved; but who, on the way to the stake, cried out to Augustine Bernher (Latimer's secretary, and the dear "companion of them that were so used"), "Oh, Austin, He is come! He is come!" It was at Coventry that Foxe met his wife. There were their own friends; their own tears were amongst the first to flow down at those blessed records.

MILES 100   200   300

Met wife at Coventry where Saunders and Glover martyred.

(J. Philpot martyred)

Foxe returned to London and completed Book of Martyrs

escape via Ipswich

exile

Frankfurt

BERLIN

GERMANY

PARIS

Basle

GENEVA

FRANCE

AUSTRIA

OLD TIMBER HOUSES, COVENTRY

To write in Latin for the learned of every nation only was not enough. Foxe burned to let his countrymen have the history all in English, that Tyndale's 'every ploughboy' also might read, hear, and know that that was the true grace of God wherein the martyrs stood, that that was the true faith for which they suffered. It was a colossal work which he undertook, but if he toiled with indefatigable zeal for years the task would be done—and he did it.

When the exiles returned, and Grindal and Pilkington and others became bishops, Foxe might have become one too, for he did not despise the office of a bishop. But because he "scrupled the habits" (disliked the surplice), and would have pressed for a further alteration in the liturgy, he was debarred from a bishopric. That clearly turned to his salvation in the work that was eminently his. He preached, it is true, at his London church in Cripplegate, and went about doing good; but having no diocesan duties he laboured hard at his book. The book, or books, contained the history of the Church in all ages. Much was taken on trust from former historians, but in giving the accounts of the martyrs who had lived and died amongst his readers, he had of course to be very certain of his ground; for "you know," he wrote, "it is not handsome to bring in doctors speaking otherwise than in their own words."

In 1582 he published the last and fullest edition of his works

John Day the Printer

JOHN DAY was still only 22 when he joined with another printer in Edward VI's time to print his first book, and for the next four years they went on working together: at first he lived just a little above Holborn conduit in London, but then he moved to Aldersgate and built the premises he needed on the old London wall.

By the time he was 30 he had a licence to print Poynet's Catechism in English, which the young Protestant king ordered to be published. Another of the little books which he printed was a sermon of Latimer's—the pages were a little smaller than this one you are reading now—and it had been preached 'in the Shrouds at St. Paul's Church in London on the 18th day of January', which means that the sermon was preached on a rainy day, and therefore not at Paul's Cross itself but in the enclosed space used for sermons in bad weather.

But too soon Edward VI died, and when Mary came to the throne, he soon found himself in prison for printing such books, and who should he find there for a friend but John Rogers who became Mary's first martyr. Yet John Rogers seemed to see the future unfold, and he promised John Day he would live to see the alteration of Mary's religion, and the gospel freely to be preached again. One day a letter was delivered to the prison for John Day, and when he read it, he found a lovely appeal from a minister named Mr. Hutchinson who was poorly in bed and dying, for him to print some more sermons of his. Listen to what John Day says: "Lying on his deathbed, he sent to me in my trouble, desiring me that whensoever Almighty God of His own mere mercy and goodness would look no more upon our wretchedness, but wipe away our sins, and hide them in the

1510	1520	1530	1540	1550	1560	1570	1580	1590

Henry VIII				E	M	Elizabeth I		
Printed the Scriptures & Reformers writings				▶■ exile		■ Printed four editions of Foxes Book of Martyrs		
		JOHN DAY, the printer						

precious wounds of His Son Jesus Christ, and turn once again His merciful countenance towards us, and lighten our hearts with the bright beams of His most glorious gospel, that I would ... put these sermons of his in print." Well, John Day did not forget his old friend's appeal, but carried it in his heart down the years till he could fulfil his wish.

John Day managed to escape abroad, and you might have thought his usefulness was almost brought to a standstill by these sad changes. But John Day was not idle: wherever he went, he kept his eyes open, learning all he could about the new methods in printing, and getting to know the young apprentices over on the Continent too. As soon as it was safe, he was back in England, and when Elizabeth came to the throne, he was quickly busy at his printing works, with boys from abroad to help him, and making many improvements in his books—he liked to see pictures where he could, and used woodcuts for this purpose; and then he was the first to print music; he printed the first collection of psalm tunes including a contribution from Tallis; he was the first to cut, cast and use Anglo-Saxon type, and very clear accurate type it was too; he introduced mathematical and other signs; he was the first to make **Roman** and *italic* types so that they could be used together in one line like this; and he was the first English printer that we have a portrait of!

He must have had a very busy home, for he married and had thirteen boys and girls before his wife died; and then he married again, and had thirteen boys and girls again, making 26 in all! but I am afraid quite a number of them

JOHN DAY

The letters at the foot of the engraving are his initials, I.D. The letters I and J were often used interchangeably, as also were the letters U and V, as will be seen in the older editions of Cruden's Concordance, for example. It was John Day's son Richard who was the first to use them separately and consistently like we do now, when he was printing books. The Latin part of the inscription round the portrait tells us it was made when he was 40 years old, and the other writing is one of his mottoes—'Life is Death and Death is Life': perhaps he was thinking of Matthew 10.39.

died before they were very old. He was the printer who did all the ABC books for the land, and I expect when they were done he would take a few home for his family.

It was not long before he printed all of Latimer's sermons, good Latimer who had been martyred in his eighties by cruel Mary; then Ridley's Friendly Farewell, and many more.

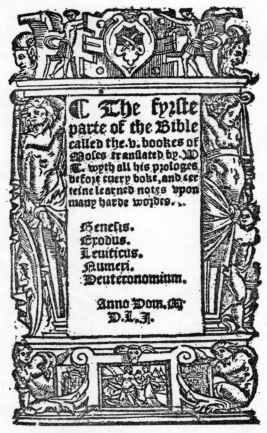

TITLE-PAGE OF THE BIBLE IN PARTS
printed by John Day

He also had the idea of printing the Bible *in parts*, so as to make it easier for people to buy them. This is how they were advertised: "Printed in sundry parts for these poor, that they which are not able to bie the hole, may bie a part."

But one of the most important of the other books he printed was John Foxe's Book of Martyrs, or to give it its full title Acts and Monuments of these latter and perilous days, touching matters of the church, wherein are comprehended and described the great persecutions and horrible troubles that have been wrought and practised by the Romish prelates, specially in this realm of England and Scotland, from the year of our Lord 1000 unto the time now present; gathered and collected according to the true copies and writings certificatory, as well of the parties themselves that suffered, as also out of the bishops' registers which were the doers thereof; by John Foxe, 1563. It had nearly 1800 folio pages; just think of all the work, and John Foxe had only had 18 months to get it ready, and even when it came out, fresh material kept arriving. For a lot of that time, Foxe travelled every Monday to John Day's printing-house, and probably lodged there most of the week. When the book was done, he sent a copy to his old college of Magdalen, Oxford.

By 1570 the second edition appeared, much enlarged— 2300 pages of double columns, with 150 woodcuts instead of 60 in the first edition. Three presses were used for the book, and John Day was hindered by a law forbidding him to employ more than four foreigners, and there were no Englishmen to do it. But a letter from Foxe to Cecil, the queen's secretary, enabled them to overcome the difficulty. Again Foxe sent one to his old college, and again they sent him a gift, and also bought two chains from the bookbinder to fasten the two volumes to their desk.

Of course, some of the cruel details regarding the treatment of the martyrs and their friends less than ten years before was bound to mention people still alive, and those with guilty consciences did not like it. For example, John Drainer was squire of Smarden in Kent, and had been angry with Gregory Dods the parson for reproving him for his evil life; so he invited Dods to breakfast to draw him out in his talk, placing one of his men, Roger Matthew, behind the door to overhear and report him. Dods was cautious however, and when Squire Drainer sent him up for heresy before the next justice, he escaped by merely being banished. Afterward Drainer himself was appointed a justice, and bored nine holes in the rood loft at Smarden church to spy out those who did not do proper obeisance when mass was celebrated, and so got the nickname Justice Nine-holes. All this was carefully reported by John Foxe in his book.

Time went by, and one day Drainer came to John Day's house with his friends, and demanded abruptly, 'Is Foxe here?' Foxe was away, so then he asked for the printer himself. Being invited in, he was asked what it was he wanted. Drainer replied that Day had printed false things about him. Being questioned further, he admitted that he *had* made five holes with an augur, and that the fresh parson had made the rest; but, he protested, you say I did it to see who worshipped the sacrament, but that is untrue. Indeed, said John Day, so we understand now, for you have been heard talking at a supper in Cheapside since, to say that you did it to look more at the pretty girls than anything. Drainer coloured, and stormed, 'Can a man speak nothing but you must have understanding of it?' Then Drainer denied once more putting a man behind his door to trap Dods in his talk. 'Oh, but it is true,' said the printer, 'for the man himself that was secretly hidden has since confessed it to Dods himself, asking his forgiveness on his knees.' 'I will hang the man,' said Drainer, and went away in a great rage; not long after he was summoned himself by death.

So you see that Foxe had been very careful and exact in writing his records, and John Day was just as careful to see that he only printed the truth.

By this time his premises were getting far too small, with his large family living there, his men working there, the books being sold there, and his stock, worth between £2000 and £3000 being kept there; so in 1572 he obtained the "lease of a little shop to be set up in St. Paul's Churchyard. Whereupon he got framed a neat, handsome shoppe. It was but little and low, and flat-roofed, and leaded like a terrace, railed and posted, fit for men to stand upon in any triumph or show." So he went on working in his long shop at the north-west corner of St. Paul's.

Printers in those days provided themselves with wonderful shop-signs, book-plates, and mottoes. Henry Bynneman, for instance, had for his sign a mermaid, and the words "Omnia tempus habent" round the edge—"All things have their time," or "There's a time for everything," How would he have carried out Foxe's orders? Probably with an orderly leisure, and 1571 would have gone by, and perhaps every other year, before there was time to consider so great a task. But John Day's sign was a man pointing a sleeper to the rising sun, and saying, "Arise, for it is day." And his motto was his daily thought: the dark night of popery had passed, the glorious gospel day had come, there was yet very much land to be possessed, and he would work while it was day. And was not such a man a gift to the nation at such a time?

But we are nearing the end of the story of good John Day. One of his sons, Richard, who went to Cambridge, was appointed vicar of Reigate in the summer of 1583, and in the summer of the next year his father died. He passed away at Walden in Essex on 23rd July aged 62, and on the 2nd August he was buried at Bradley Parva in Suffolk, where there is monumental brass to his memory. It seems that

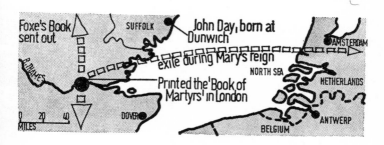

Richard now left Reigate to carry on the printing business for a time.

Another son, John (1566-1628) became one of the most frequent and noted preachers in the University of Oxford, adhering strongly to the Calvinistic doctrines his father had loved and taught him; and later became a minister at Little Thurlow in Suffolk until his death; then it was that another brother Lionel, who tells us that he was the only survivor of all those 26 children, put up a monument to his brother's memory there.

The Fire and the Pestilence

THERE was a great concourse of people at St. Paul's Cross on the afternoon of the Lord's day, June 8th 1561. The Cathedral had been burnt on the previous Wednesday, fire breaking out in the steeple and consuming a great part of the building. Dr. Grindal, the Bishop of London, had appointed the good Bishop of Durham to preach at the Cross about it. In his sermon Dr. Pilkington spoke of the calamity as a judgment, and there was not a man, woman or child who listened to him who thought of it as anything else. Not to acknowledge God's hand in events is an atheism that was very uncommon in those days.

But what the people wanted to hear as they sat or stood round St. Paul's Cross was *why* the calamity had been sent. The Bishop preached a long sermon, for during the past four days many reasons had been discussed. Some said that it was because of the Reformation, the new Bible reading, the new protestantism and preaching. "No," said Dr. Pilkington, "it is not that. St. Paul's has been burnt down twice before, in the very midst of the reign of popery; once in the first year of King Stephen's reign, and once in the reign of Henry VI."

Another reason given was that the Cathedral had been made a den of thieves. Yes, it had; walking about, jangling, brawling, fighting and bargaining as if it was a market-place, had gone on during sermon and service time. That was a great evil. But another reason given was the sins and iniquities in general of—other people. "No," said Dr. Pilkington, "do not assign the cause to other men's sins, but let each one say with David, 'I am the man,' and turn from his own evil ways, for unless there is restitution of ill-gotten goods and a reformation in various other ways, a greater plague will be sent." He said that if the people acknowledged God, they would not seek superstitious means of escape in cases of fire, such as calling upon St. Agatha and using various charms. It was God, he said, who made and gave them good things, and who guides, rules, feeds and increases all; and they should not call out, "St. Anthony, save my hog," "St. Loy, save my horse," "St. Blaze, save my house," "St. Apollony, cure my tooth-ache," but acknowledge God in all

OLD ST. PAUL'S CROSS

	1558	1559	1560	1561	1562	1563
	MARY I	ELIZABETH I				
		St. Pauls Cathedral Fire >		London Pestilence >		
		Dr. Pilkington's Sermon >		John Foxe's letter >		
Act of Uniformity >		Bishop Grindal gives living to Coverdale >				

these things; they should let popish superstitions go, and turn to God's Word now open for their hearing. And Bishop Pilkington prayed, "Lord, open the hearts of Thy people, that they may see how far more acceptable to Thee is the lively preaching of Thy holy Word than all the glittering ceremonies of popery."

After two years, in 1563, a pestilence swept London.

Those in high places had not learned all that Bishop Pilkington would have them learn from his great sermon at St. Paul's Cross two years before. The mayor, aldermen and rich merchants hurried to their country houses and left the city to its fate. Masters closed their shops and took their families away, leaving the shopmen, apprentices and errand boys without work and without wages. There was starvation and want, and twenty thousand people died by the plague.

During that time many ministers went about doing good. London was by no means short of good ministers although other places were woefully so. One minister, John Foxe (the immortal martyrologist) wrote a letter to the aldermen of the city saying that he could not see that they were justified by the Word of God in flying from their needy neighbours without sending help to them, that the aldermen ought to feel it as much their duty to remain in the city as the ministers to remain in their parishes. "What do your scarlet robes mean," he wrote, "if not that you are ready to defend your people with your blood? Is running away being ready to give your lives for them? What can be said when you simply give them no help at all?"

Now things of that kind show that it was not all "Merrie England" in the days of Queen Bess; our councillors do not nowadays leave the poor unprovided for. But improvement came as God's Word prevailed. Here and there all over the country, men of power and wealth were to be found, richly endued with the Spirit of Christ, the salt of society, blessed, godly and munificent. At the end of the reign of Queen Elizabeth, the aldermen of the city would no more have thought of leaving the Londoners in the lurch than they would now. Things had changed for the better.

It was during that year of pestilence 1563 that Bishop Grindal in one particular case set aside the Act of Uniformity. Miles Coverdale of all people was under the ban of the Act because of his Puritan opinions. He was living in London, an old man and in great poverty. He had been preaching it is true, but as if by stealth and as a "silenced" minister; people had been accustomed to go to the door of his house on Saturdays to ask at which house he was to preach on the following day, and the place of meeting was constantly changed for fear of detection. But now Grindal determined to give him the living of St. Magnus the Martyr, London Bridge. This he did, but not without having to assure Archbishop Parker that the step was right in the sight of God. "He was in Christ before us," he told Parker. When Coverdale entered again upon his labours in the pulpit great crowds flocked to hear him. They knew their old friend Coverdale, the great translator of the Bible; they had often heard him preach at St. Paul's Cross.

Coverdale and Grindal had long been friends. They were both ardent reformers and desired to have a pure scriptural

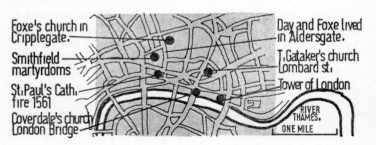

Foxe's church in Cripplegate.

Smithfield martyrdoms

St. Paul's Cath. fire 1561

Coverdale's church London Bridge

Day and Foxe lived in Aldersgate.

T. Gataker's church Lombard st.

Tower of London

RIVER THAMES.

ONE MILE

church. Coverdale preferred to lose preferment while a rag of popery remained. Grindal was afraid that if all the chief reformers did so there would be no bishop left to keep out the arch-enemy, popery. And so he accepted the bishopric of London, and until that dark year of the pestilence, he had enforced the Act and carried out the Queen's wishes. But now brotherly kindness and love overcame that stiff enforcement, and Coverdale was allowed to preach and conduct the services in St. Magnus church as he thought best.

Archbishop Parker and Bishop Grindal differed greatly; the Archbishop enforced the Act with more rigour as time went on, but Grindal with less. He was a man of prayer; he looked upon preaching as the power of God unto salvation; he saw all things at the sovereign, merciful and righteous disposal of the eternal, just, omnipotent and gracious God. He knew that that gracious God could remove the pestilence that year with a word, but could not bear the thought that His servant Miles Coverdale was in the stricken city, but unable to lift up his voice in preaching to the living, dying *people* of the city.

Back in 1564, John Day the printer had published the letters that some of the martyrs of Mary's days had written, and Miles Coverdale had written the Address to the Reader, to go at the front of it. This is what he wrote to encourage people to read the letters:

'Because in such writings, as in a clear glass, we may see and behold not only what plentiful furniture and store of heavenly grace, wisdom, knowledge, understanding, faith, love, hope, zeal, patience, meekness, obedience, with the worthy fruits thereof, almighty God had bestowed upon the same his most dear children; but also what a fatherly care he ever had unto them; how his mighty hand defended them; how his providence kept watch and ward over them; how his loving eye looked unto them; how his gracious care heard their prayers; how he was always mindful of them, never forgot them, neither failed them nor forsook them; how the arms of his mercy were stretched out to embrace them whenever they faithfully turned unto him; how valiant also and strong in spirit, how joyful under the cross, how quiet and cheerful in trouble he made them; what victory over their enemies, what deliverance out of bonds and captivity, what health from sickness, what recovery from plagues, what plenty from scarceness; to be short, what help at all need and necessity he gave and bestowed upon them.'

Well, so Miles Coverdale had proved it to be at the end. His great life's work had been his translation of the Bible, so we will take our leave of him by listening to his advice:

'Now I will exhort thee, whoever thou be that readest scripture, if thou find ought therein that thou understandest not, or that appeareth to be repugnant, given no rash or hasty judgment thereof: but ascribe it to thine own ignorance, not to the scripture; ... it shall greatly help thee to understand scripture if thou mark not only what is spoken or written, but of whom, and unto whom, with what words, at what time, where, to what intent, with what circumstance, considering what goes before, and what follows after. For there be some things which are done and written to the intent that we should do likewise, as when Abraham believes God, is obedient unto his word, and defends Lot his kinsman from violent wrong. There be some things also which are written, to the intent we should eschew (avoid) suchlike, as when David lies with Uriah's wife, and causes him to be slain. Therefore, I say, when thou readest scripture, be wise and circumspect. ... Now to conclude: forsomuch as all the scripture is written for thy doctrine and example, it shall be necessary for thee to take hold upon it while it is offered thee, yea, and with ten hands thankfully to receive it.'

Mr. Greenham's Harvest

ONE Summer early in the reign of Queen Elizabeth, as in many others of the sixteenth century, there was little prospect of a good harvest. Many a farmer of no better morals than his fellows, felt glad when he received a message from the Clerk of the Market, to send in his bushel measure, in order that a piece might be cut off the top of it. The Clerk of the Market had public orders to do this; it was quite the custom in a district threatened with a food shortage. The bushel measures were made smaller and returned to their owners, all alike, but not full bushels. And so in that season, not only was the price of the corn very high, but the poor housewives found that when the miller had ground their bushel of corn into flour, their loaves were smaller than they ought to have been.

But in the year of our story the Clerk did not have it altogether his own way. Mr. Richard Greenham of Dry Drayton near Cambridge, had glebe lands. He was accustomed to sell his surplus corn but he would not allow his man to take the bushel measure to be cut down. This exasperated the Clerk of the Market and Mr. Greenham got into some trouble for it, "but," says the writer of his Life, "the Lord delivered him out of the snare."

In that heavy season the poor of Dry Drayton fared much better than the poor of other villages; their corn was less than half the price, and they had "good measure, pressed down," because Mr. Greenham often told his men not to strike off all the corn above the rim. His way of bringing about this plenty in the midst of dearth was a very simple one. Dry Drayton had had its parish priests for years; they had the same glebe lands, and there had been bad seasons in which their people fared no better than others. But Mr.

1530	1540	1550	1560	1570	1580	1590	1600	1610
Henry VIII		E₁	M	Elizabeth I				James I
				▶ Dry Drayton yrs. ◀				
	Richard Greenham							

Greenham had a book which his predecessors had never cared to consult, although it contained simple directions how to act in such a case. I need not say it was the Bible. If the supplies of food for his poor people were very small, he read, "Bring them hither to Me." He read about Joseph laying up the corn in readiness for the famine, and he simply did that very thing; *he induced twenty farmers to lay up corn in a common granary,* each putting in what he was willing to spare, and he himself putting in much more than any of them. Then he appointed a certain ration for each family, and Dry Drayton was tided over the dearth.

After seasons of scarcity the want and poverty in some places were often so great that many of the poor turned to

'Twenty farmers lay up corn in a common granary'

begging and wandering. The number of beggars in the country was enormous, but Dry Drayton added none to their number that year.

I can imagine a remark from one who dislikes the thought of the Reformation:—"What an iniquitous public order, to cut the measure down! and under your Protestant rule! I thought you boasted that a greater integrity came with the Reformation." Yes; but not by magic, or as a child might imagine, viz., that a good king or queen arose, and on that day every bad custom stopped and every good one was created and appeared. In Green's illustrated *Short History* there is a reproduction of the mottoes and devices of the bakers of York. Some of the measures appear to be made of leather, and round the quaint pictures is printed:

> "He that giveth measure
> God blesseth with treasure;
> Be just with thy weights,
> God plagueth false sleights.
> Whoso followeth these precepts well,
> God blesseth their labour
> With plenty and favour."

But the date of these devices is 1595, much nearer the end than the beginning of Queen Elizabeth's reign; and Mr. Greenham's life in Dry Drayton helps to show *how* we got our national integrity, or how we got it back after it had been besmirched with the blight of popery. Richard Greenham did not leave his people without definite teaching about the dishonesty of cutting down the bushel measure. It was his custom to preach on Mondays, Tuesdays, Wednesdays and Fridays, very early in the morning in summer, and as soon as it was light enough to see in winter, and he always had a good congregation. Many, perhaps most or all of them, heard his texts for the first time in their lives: "A false balance is abomination to the Lord, but a just weight is His delight." "Hear this, O ye that swallow up the needy, even to make the poor of the land to fail, saying, When will the new moon be gone, that we may sell corn? and the Sabbath, that we may set forth wheat, making the ephah small and the shekel great, and falsifying the balances by deceit?" He preached with great fervour, and always went home on these early mornings like a workman from his toil. He had been up since four o'clock to read and pray before preaching, but it suited the people to go to church before their work began. That was an "early service" with some point in its timing!

Often during his twenty years at Dry Drayton he was to be seen taking a walk in the fields in the afternoon and stopping to talk to the ploughmen or reapers. To some of them this was delightful; to others, irritating. It was either love or hatred with the Dry Drayton people. When in 1589 Mr. Greenham left them and went to London, some of them were peculiarly obstinate in ungodliness, and bitter against the one who, like Bunyan's Evangelist, had "offered to turn them into the way." Yet he had not lorded it over the heritage; on the contrary, while some of them grudged him his house and land, his liberality left little for his own needs. His wife was about to pay their own reapers one harvest-time, when lo! there was no money. Her husband had given the last of it away and she had to borrow.

Mrs. Greenham had been the widow of one whose name became well known in connection with keeping holy the Lord's day—Dr. Nicholas Bound. Dr. Bound's book on the Sabbath was cried down and suppressed by powerful High Churchmen, but the more it was attacked the more it spread; and more and more the custom grew of keeping the day holy and free, not only from unnecessary work, but from those recreations which are lawful on other days. The book spread, and was discussed after Mr. Greenham's death; but in the preaching and practice of both these good men we have another example of how we got our English Sabbath. Indeed, we read of Mr. Greenham's book on the Sabbath as well as of Dr. Bound's.

For generations fairs and markets were held in many churchyards on the Lord's day. Against that, there had been some show of zeal for God's honour, even in popish times. In 1416, for instance, there was a bye-law in York that no market "sholde be holden by vytaylers and other chapmen on Sondaye ne in ye Sentuary ne out" (no market should be held by victuallers and other hawkers on Sundays either in the church or in the churchyard). In 1268 a similar law had been passed at the Synod of London.

The land had enjoyed her Sabbaths in some places when the gospel first came to Britain, and again it may be in such days as when Ina, King of Wessex, made a law that if a lord caused his slave to work on the Sabbath he should pay a fine; if the slave worked without his lord's command he should "pay it with his skin." King Alfred ruled in all godliness, and Edgar the Peaceful—though superstition was growing apace in his century, the tenth—ruled that the Sabbath should be kept from noon on Saturday till dawn on Monday. Possibly that is why, to this day, the servant is in so many cases free from his master on Saturday afternoon. Perhaps Edgar was wise above what is written in his enactment; he certainly was, if he meant, "Five and a half days shalt thou labour, and do all thy work." But whether it was so or not, laws continued to be enacted, but never enforced, and so centuries had gone by, and popery had its ripe fruit in Tudor times—early mass and a noisy day.

It may be however that the Saxon king had the idea of the day of preparation in his mind, and that he thought it best that his subjects should bake what they would bake that day, and seethe what they would seethe (Exod. 16), and that was certainly a great point with the Puritans.

Mr. Greenham's step-daughter, Anne Bound, was married to a Puritan minister whose preaching drew people from many distant villages. "He was given to hospitality, delighting therein, keeping a constant table on the Sabbath, upon which days he had not less than eight or twelve persons commonly dining with him, and he spent the time amongst them in spiritual exhortation and conference" (Samuel Clark). When any of these strangers hesitated to trespass on his hospitality, he assured them that a very ample amount of food had been prepared the day before.

It was not however in the matter of work only, that the Puritans wished for a reformation in Sabbath-keeping. Dr. Bound's prohibition of amusements drew down the displeasure of the High Church party. The Queen was fond of watching plays on Lord's day evenings. Outdoor sports of all kinds were carried on everywhere. Many clergymen and bishops played bowls in the afternoon. The opposers of the Puritans contended that in forbidding recreation they were turning Englishmen into Old Testament Jews. But their reply to that charge was that the Sabbath was "from the beginning," and that the Lord's day like the old Sabbath was the day for worship; that games are suitable as recreation to fit people for coming work but not for coming worship. And so Mr. Greenham did not suffer the people of his charge to dance and skip on the green on the Lord's day, and he was hated on that account by those of them who liked to do so.

But outward reformation was not the ultimate aim in his ministry. Some of those ploughmen and reapers who were glad when he came to the fields and talked with them, "groaned under spiritual afflictions and temptations," and he came and often comforted them. Others had already been delivered from their greatest fears through his preaching, and were ready to hear and to praise the Lord for His goodness. The work of the Holy Spirit was extremely powerful in His people's hearts, both in wounding and in binding up, and many of his hearers were "restored to joy and comfort out of unspeakable and insupportable terrors and torments of conscience" (Clark). Their minister's heart and mind were taken up in sympathy with them. People in distress of soul, rich and poor, came from distant places to

Hildersham preached at Ashby-de-la-Zouch 1587–1632

LEICESTERSHIRE

CAMBRIDGESHIRE

Richard Greenham at Dry Drayton 1569–89 died in London 1591

RIVER SEVERN

0   20   40
MILES

Dr. Chadderton master at Emmanuel College Cambridge 1583–1622

T. Gataker preached in London until 1593

confer with him. His hospitality to them—for days or weeks—was the incidental accompaniment of his giving himself to be theirs, and of his seeking, not theirs, but them. His laying up corn for his people, supplying them with good measure, and the resultant happy harvest at Dry Drayton, were an emblem of the spiritual harvest that followed his sojourn there. Possibly the harvest of his ministry is not yet past. He wrote "Comfort for an Afflicted Conscience," and some other treatises, and C. H. Spurgeon has incorporated some of his writings in his exposition of Psalm 119. He lived only two years in London, and died worn out with his labours in 1591, in the sixtieth year of his age—a shock of corn fully ripe.

On one occasion Mr. Greenham had to appear before the Bishop of Ely, because of some point of nonconformity. The Bishop asked him where the blame was to be laid—on the conformists or the nonconformists; to which he answered that it might be on either side or on neither. He had seen a good deal of episcopal tyranny, and he had also seen the tracts of Martin Marprelate which showed up that tyranny; but which, as he said, made sin which should appear odious appear only ridiculous. He was so thankful for the amount of liberty there was, compared with the sufferings that were inflicted in Queen Mary's reign, that it was a great theme with him; he never could get over the wonderful and happy deliverances that came in with Queen Elizabeth, and his thoughts were much taken up with it the day before he died.

There we might leave Mr. Greenham, but that the date of his death, 1591, coincides with the "harvest" of another man—poor Sir Christopher Hatton. He had lived flattering Queen Elizabeth, and so basking in her capricious smiles, that he said it was his heaven to serve her. She had once acquired "Hatton Garden" as a kind of Naboth's vineyard, and given it to him; but at last he fell under her displeasure, and it was said that he died of grief. "In the day shalt thou make thy plant to grow, and in the morning shalt thou make thy seed to flourish; but the harvest shall be a heap in the day of grief and of desperate sorrow" (Isaiah 17.11).

Before we leave Richard Greenham, we will just peep over his shoulder. He has Psalm 119 open in front of him, and he is writing out his explanations of each verse; see, he has reached verse 7, Learned thy righteous judgments—so he picks up his pen: 'We see here what David especially desired to learn, namely, the word and will of God: he would ever be a scholar in this school, and sought daily to ascend to the highest form; that learning to know, he might remember; remembering, might believe; believing, might delight; delighting, might admire; admiring, might adore; adoring, might practise; and practising, might continue in the way of God's statutes.' He reaches verse 26, Teach me thy statutes; again his pen travels over the paper—'The oft repetition of this one thing in this psalm argues, 1. The necessity of this knowledge; 2. The desire he had to obtain it; 3. That such repetitions are not frivolous when they proceed from a sound heart, a zealous affection, and a consideration of the necessity of the thing prayed for; 4. That such as have most light have little in respect of what they should have; 5. As covetous men think they never have enough gold, so Christian men should think they never have enough knowledge.'

He studies verse 65, Thou hast dealt well with thy servant. And so he sets down: 'He knew that God's gifts are without repentance, and that he is not weary of well-doing, but will finish the thing he hath begun; and therefore he pleads past favours. Here is a difference between faith and an accusing conscience: the accusing conscience is afraid to ask more, because it has abused the former mercies; but faith, assuring us that all God's benefits are tokens of his love bestowed on us according to his word, is bold to ask for more.'

And eventually what he wrote on that psalm took up pages 379 to 608 in his works printed in 1612!

Archbishop Grindal and the Prophesyings

DR. GRINDAL landed in England from exile on the Queen's Coronation Day in 1559, with Dr. Sandys, who in spite of the general rejoicing said that they had come back to sorrow. It was a grief of mind to them that there were divisions among the Protestants. Had they known that their right course would have been to let Puritans and Separatists enjoy their own forms of worship, both of them might have been spared much sorrow.

Edmund Grindal came from Cumberland, and was so fond of books when he was a boy that he often carried one with him when he was out walking on his own. One day going through a field with a book stuffed in his half-buttoned-up coat, an arrow struck right on the book, and so his life was saved from an accidental death.

When he grew older, he became one of Ridley's chaplains in Edward VI's days: but when the dreaded reign of Mary began, he escaped to Germany. Now he was back again.

In 1576 Grindal became Archbishop of Canterbury, and had a deeper cause for sadness than any regret that his views of worship were not shared by all good Englishmen. Almost immediately the Queen gave him to understand that she wanted to put down preaching—the very preaching of the gospel. And why should not his countenance be sad when the city of Jerusalem over which he was set as watchman, was threatened with so great a desolation?

It may seem strange that Queen Elizabeth objected to preaching and laid a command upon the man who by her own royal favour had just been advanced. While some writers put it down to a bias in her mind which appeared in a lingering fondness for the religion of her fathers, the historian Fuller tells us that it was the work of Grindal's enemies, two of the Queen's favourites—the Earl of Leicester and Sir Christopher Hatton. "His fault was keeping others from breaking two of God's commandments—'Thou shalt not steal,' when he would not let the Lord of Leicester have Lambeth House, and 'Thou shalt not commit adultery,' when he would not permit Julio, the Earl's Italian physician, to marry another man's wife."

Needless to say, the Earl did not bring these as charges against Grindal and neither did Sir Christopher Hatton bring a charge against him; they worked more "wilily." The summer of 1575 had been the time of the Queen's great visit to the Earl of Leicester at Kenilworth, and Sir Christopher Hatton was one of those most continually at her side. The unparalleled splendour of that royal progress has been celebrated in romance. It passed, and they returned to London, with all the grandeur and gaiety to look back upon. It had been an uninterrupted round of pleasure and even after they had attended Her Majesty on the Lord's day mornings to hear "fruitful" sermons, the fruit they enjoyed with her in the afternoons of the sacred day was dancing, bear-baiting, masques, and plays.

It was at this juncture that Grindal was appointed to the vacant see of Canterbury. Archbishop Parker, who had died early in the year was one who himself gave feasts and entertainments on the Lord's day; and it was not to be endured by the courtiers that his successor should set an example of godliness, or recommend to Her Majesty court preachers who would expose the vanity and sin of worldliness.

It was somewhat difficult to attack preaching in general, but Sir Christopher Hatton obtained his wish by attacking what were called the 'Prophesyings.' These were not the ordinary Lord's day sermons, but conferences held on weekdays in churches. Several ministers in turn spoke from one text, and a moderator 'summed up and closed the exercise,' which was carried on in the presence of large and interested audiences. They could not but be popular in days when there was a spirit of eager enquiry and no religious magazines. They were not mere debates, but naturally many a knotty point of controversy was discussed.

Now because there had been occasion for regulating the Prophesyings, so that due order might be observed in the gatherings, and because Grindal had been a great upholder of them (whereas Archbishop Parker had hated them), his two enemies found in this a pretext for insinuating to the Queen that she little knew what hot-beds of sedition and political plotting the Prophesyings were. Had not Archbishop Parker only a short time before counselled her to have them suppressed in the diocese of Norwich? Elizabeth lent a ready ear to the insinuation, having good reason to dislike plots. She sent for Grindal and asked him personally to put an end to the Prophesyings. She could not allow seditious gatherings or have mere lay people unnecessarily instructed. She added that there was now far too much preaching in general; three or four sermons in a year were quite enough for any congregation. He would therefore see to it that reading the Homilies was substituted for preaching throughout the country. Such was her wish, and it was for him to carry it out.

The Archbishop went from Her Majesty's presence sorrowful. There was no truth in calling the Prophesyings seditious. He had already regulated them by rules as simple as might be enforced nowadays—each speaker keeping to his proper turn, no political topic being allowed, no countenance given to rowdy interruptions. But the greatest sting was in the last

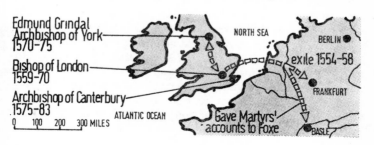

Edmund Grindal
Archbishop of York
1570-75

Bishop of London
1559-70

Archbishop of Canterbury
1575-83

NORTH SEA

BERLIN

exile 1554-58

FRANKFURT

ATLANTIC OCEAN

Gave Martyrs' accounts to Foxe

BASLE

0   100   200   300 MILES

part of the Queen's request: the command that they should hardly speak at all nor teach in the Name of the Lord Jesus. Grindal wrote a letter to the Queen, long and wordy (as so much writing was in those days), but the following is a curtailed version of it:—

To her Majesty.   December 20th, 1576.

With most humble remembrance of my bounden duty to Your Majesty, the speeches it hath pleased you to deliver me concerning abridging the number of preachers and the utter suppression of conferences among ministers, have exceedingly dismayed and discomforted me. Alas, Madam, is the Scripture more plain in any one thing than that the gospel of Christ should be plentifully preached? To the building of Solomon's material temple there were appointed a hundred and fifty thousand labourers and three hundred overseers, and shall we think a few preachers may suffice to edify the spiritual temple of Christ? St. Paul said, "Preach the word, be instant in season, out of season," and the apostles appointed elders in every church, men who by sound doctrine should convince the gainsayers. I beseech Your Majesty to note one thing, that if the Holy Ghost prescribe expressly, that preachers should be placed in every town or city, how can it well be thought that three or four preachers may suffice for a shire? Public and continual preaching of God's word is the ordinary instrument of salvation. By preaching also, obedience to magistrates is planted in the hearts of subjects, and no prince ever had more experience of this than Your Majesty.

If Your Majesty come to the city of London never so often, what joy and concourse of people is seen, what prayers for your long life! Whereof cometh this but by the continual preaching of God's word in the city? On the contrary, what bred the rebellion in the North?—papistry and ignorance of God's word. And in the time of that rebellion were not men that made profession of the gospel the most ready in your defence, insomuch that one poor parish (Halifax I mean) was ready to bring three or four thousand men against the rebels?

That unable preachers be removed is requisite, and I trust that therein as much is done as can be. For my own part I am very careful in allowing only such as be able for their knowledge in the scriptures and for the testimony of their good lives; we admit no man to the office that either professeth papistry or puritanism. Generally only graduates of the university are admitted to be preachers, unless it be some few who have excellent gifts of knowledge in the scriptures, joined with good utterance and godly persuasion. I myself procured about forty learned preachers and graduates within less than six years, to be placed within the diocese of York, besides these I found therein,—the fruits of whose travelling preaching Your Majesty is like to reap daily, by most assured dutiful obedience of your subjects in those parts. But indeed this age judgeth very hardly of the ability of preachers of our time, judging few or none to be able; and that hard judgment groweth upon the evil disposition of man. St. Paul commands the preaching of Christ crucified, without excellency of speech, but in our time many have so delicate ears that no preaching can satisfy them, unless it be sauced with much fineness and exornation of speech, which the same apostle utterly condemns, lest the cross of Christ be made of none effect. Some mislike the godly Reformation, and, wishing there were no preachers, deprave the ministers by secret undermining, much like the popish bishops in your father's time, who would have had the English translation of the Bible called in, as evil translated, and the new translation committed to themselves—which they never intended to perform. Some serve mammon, not God; a great many are lovers of pleasure more than of God, and preaching, to their seared consciences, is bitter; and they too, daring not openly to condemn the preaching of God's word (for that were open blasphemy) take exceptions against them that be admitted to preach.

But God forbid, Madam, that you should open your ears to these wicked persuasions. Now, where it is thought that the reading of godly homilies set forth by public authority may suffice, I continue of the mind that it hath its commodity but is nothing comparable to the office of preaching. They were devised by the godly bishops in your brother's time only to supply necessity, for want of preachers, and were never thought to contain sufficient instruction for the church of England, but only that half a loaf is better than no bread.

Now for the part concerning the learned exercises and conferences among the ministers. I have consulted with divers of my brethren the bishops by letters, who think as I do, that they are profitable for the church, and expedient to be continued. I trust Your Majesty will think the like when Your Highness is informed what authority it hath in the Scriptures, and what commodity it bringeth.

The bishops have authority to appoint these exercises, and once a month for two hours in the church some text before appointed is interpreted. The occasion and end is showed, the proper sense, the propriety of the words, and in the tongues, the diversities of interpretations. It is shown where like phrases are used in Scripture, and places seeming to contradict each other are reconciled; the arguments are opened, virtues and vices touched upon and pointed out, and they show to which of the commandments they pertain. It is shown how the text hath been wrested by adversaries, and what doctrine of faith and manners it contains. In conclusion there is the prayer for Your Majesty and all estates, and a psalm. The order is also observed that two or three of the gravest and best learned pastors are appointed by the bishops to moderate in every assembly.

The ground of these exercises is of ancient authority. Samuel did practise the like in Ramatha and Bethel; so did Elizeus at Jericho; St. Paul also doth mention that the like in effect was used in the primitive church and gives rules that two or three should speak and the rest keep silence. That exercise in those days Paul calleth Prophecy, not to signify prediction of things to come, but (by consent of the best ancient writers) the interpretation and exposition of Scripture, and therefore doth Paul attribute to those prophets "doctrine, edification, exhortation and comfort." The gift of interpretation was then given by miracle, without study, but

EDMUND GRINDAL

now, miracles ceasing, men must attain to the knowledge of Hebrew, Greek and Latin by travel and study, God giving the increase. So must men also attain to the gift of expounding and interpretation and amongst other helps nothing is so necessary as these conferences amongst ministers. We have found the ministers apter to teach their flocks. Nothing by experience beateth down popery more than that ministers grow to such good knowledge by means of these exercises, and where, afore there were not three able preachers, now thirty are meet to preach at Paul's Cross. Only backward men in religion and contemners of learning do fret against it; the dissolution of it would breed triumph to the adversaries and great sorrow to the favourers of religion, contrary to the counsel of Ezekiel who saith the heart of the righteous must not be made sad. And although some few have abused this good and necessary exercise there is no reason that the malice of a few should prejudice all. There is likewise no just cause of offence if divers men make divers senses of one sentence of scripture so that all the senses be agreeable to the analogy of faith.

I trust when Your Majesty hath considered, you will rest satisfied that no such inconvenience can grow of these exercises as you have been informed, but rather the contrary. I cannot with safe conscience and without the offence of the majesty of God give my consent to their suppressing—"I can do nothing against the truth, but for the truth." If it please Your Majesty for any other cause to remove me out of this place I will with all humility yield. I consider with myself that it is a fearful thing to fall into the hands of the living God and what should I win if I gained the whole world and lose my own soul? Bear with me, I beseech you, Madam, if I choose rather to offend your earthly Majesty than to offend the heavenly Majesty of God. When you deal in matters of faith and religion my petition is that you use not to pronounce too resolutely and peremptorily, as you may do in civil matters. But always remember the will of God (and not of a creature) is to take place. It is the antichristian voice of the Pope, "So I will have it." David exhorteth all kings to serve God with fear and trembling. Remember, Madam, that you are a mortal creature. Look not upon the princely array wherewith you are apparelled—what is it that is covered? is it not flesh and blood? is it not dust and ashes? is it not a corruptible body which must return to earth again God knows how soon? must not you also appear one day before the fearful judgment seat of the Crucified, to receive there according as you have done in the body, whether it be good or evil? Wherefore I beseech you, Madam, *in visceribus Christi,* when you deal in these religious causes, let the majesty of God be before your eyes and say, "Not mine but Thy will be done." God hath blessed you with great felicity in your reign—give God the glory; impute your said felicity (for instruments and means) first to the goodness of the cause you have set forth, I mean Christ's true religion, and secondly to the sighs and groanings of the godly in their fervent prayer to God for you. Take heed that you never once think of declining from God, lest that be verified of you which is written of Joash, who continued a prince of good government for many years, and when he was strengthened, his heart was lifted up to his destruction, and he regarded not the Lord. You have done many things well, but except you persevere to the end you cannot be blessed. But if you turn from God, then God will turn away His merciful countenance from you. And what remaineth then to be looked for but only a terrible expectation of God's judgments and an heaping up wrath against the day of wrath?

But I trust in God Your Majesty will always humble yourself under His mighty hand and go forward in the zealous setting forth of God's true religion. And if you do so, although God hath just cause many ways to be angry with you and us for unfaithfulness, yet I doubt not but that for His Own Name's sake and for His glory's sake He will still hold His merciful hand over us, shield and protect us under the shadow of His wings as He hath done hitherto.

I beseech God our heavenly Father plentifully to pour His principal Spirit upon you, and always to direct your heart in His holy fear. Amen."

Grindal's letter offended the Queen; like Jeremiah he was shut up in the court of the prison—his own house— and the Prophesyings were put down. Neal in his 'History of the Puritans' says that they were never revived. That is not quite accurate. Tobie Matthew Bishop of Durham revived them in his diocese, and although they ceased to be carried on under the guidance of bishops in other dioceses, the Puritans' market day lectures in later times were very like them. For years after their suppression there was a growing perception amongst godly people of what they had lost.

One of London's most worthy citizens, Sir Robert Cotton, contrasted 'the old days' with dark days that followed, and sighed for the times of the Prophesyings, saying, "In those

1520	1530	1540	1550	1560	1570	1580	1590	1600

Henry VIII   E M   Elizabeth I

exile | Bishop of London | Letter to Queen Archbishop of York then Canterbury

Edmund Grindal

days there was an emulation between the clergy and the laity, and a strife whether of them should show themselves most affectionate to the gospel. Ministers haunted the houses of the worthiest men where Jesuits now build their tabernacles; and poor country churches were frequented with the best of the shire. The word of God was precious, prayer and preaching went hand in hand together, until Archbishop Grindal's disgrace and Hatton's hard conceit of prophesying brought the flowing of these good graces to a still water."*

Now during these years, although the Queen parcelled out very many of his duties to others, and obliged him to ask permission to go even from London to Croydon, Grindal was not deprived of his right to give licences to preach. And it was to PURITAN ministers his last licences were given. The suppression of the Prophesyings in the diocese of Norwich, already mentioned, had been carried out ruthlessly over the head of its very godly bishop—Bishop Parkhurst. Parkhurst's affection was very much with the Puritans, and scores of them preached constantly in their churches unmolested. But Bishop Parkhurst died in 1575, and under a severe successor the Puritans were suspended and deprived. In 1577 they sent a petition to Archbishop Grindal, and he gave them licence to preach in any place whatever throughout the diocese, provided only that they did not deliberately preach against ceremonies and habits, a restraint which some men of peace voluntarily observed.

No attempt was made as Grindal had feared to limit preachers to three or four sermons a year. God did not suffer

* E. Middleton, Biographica Evangelica

the great enemy of souls thus to bring back the arid wastes of popery, nor "stay the bottles of heaven." In 1583 the Queen relented towards Grindal. Fuller says, "Being nearly blind, more with grief than age, he was willing to put off his clothes before he went to bed, and in his life-time to resign his post to Dr. Whitgift, who refused such acceptance thereof. And the Queen, commiserating his condition, was graciously pleased to say that, as she had made him, so he should die, an Archbishop."

Grindal was not naturally a John Knox who never feared the face of man or queen. Nor was he like his friend Foxe, who because he "scrupled the habits," that is, objected to surplices, refused a bishopric and remained poor. But we read of King Asa that "the high places were not taken away out of Israel, nevertheless the heart of Asa was perfect all his days." Grindal's heart was with the godly. Toplady calls him "a prelate in whom the whole assembly of Christian graces met." Scarcely any in his time thought toleration right; he unwillingly but at the same time conscientiously 'silenced' clergymen who did not comply in all particulars with the Act of Uniformity. The Independents he thought an unhappy faction, to be severely punished. But he felt an increasing grief in persecuting, and a decreasing fear of royal displeasure, and he was found at the last like Nicodemus, regardless of the frowns of men, in the cause of his blessed Redeemer.

I am sure that Grindal must have often been consoled by singing one of the psalms of Sternhold and Hopkins' version—perhaps Psalm 130, put into verse by William Whittingham, of whom we read on page 43:

> Lord, unto thee I make my moan
> When dangers me oppress;
> I call, I sigh, complain and groan,
> Trusting to find release.
>
> Hearken, O Lord, to my request,
> Unto my suit incline,
> And let thine ears, O Lord, be pressed
> To hear this prayer of mine.

O Lord our God, if thou survey
   Our sins, and them peruse,
Who shall escape? or who dare say,
   I can myself excuse?

But thou art merciful and free,
   And boundless in thy grace,
That we might always careful be
   To fear before thy face.

In God the Lord I put my trust,
   My soul waits on his will;
His promise is for ever just,
   And I hope therein still.

My soul to God hath great regard,
   Wishing for him alway:
Much more than they that watch and ward
   To see the dawning day.

O Israel, trust in the Lord,
   With him there mercy is,
And he doth plenteously afford
   Redemption unto his.

E'en he it is that Israel shall,
   Through his abundant grace,
Redeem from his offences all,
   And wholly them deface.

William Perkins

1. AT THE GALLOWS

WILLIAM PERKINS, who died in the last year of the reign of Queen Elizabeth, was born in the first year of it at Marston in Warwickshire. Before his conversion he lived a reckless, wicked life, according to the wickedness practised by young gentlemen in those days, for he came to Christ's College, Cambridge, and I am sorry to say he often got drunk. One day, while he was walking on the outskirts of the town, he heard a mother saying to her awkward child, "Keep your tongue still or I'll give you to drunken Perkins over there." To find himself the talk of the town was the first thing that made him think about the state of his soul. He could not rest, until he was brought to know that his sins were forgiven and that he had peace with God through the Lord Jesus Christ. Another heart *changed for the better*.

By the time he was twenty-four years old, he was "clothed and in his right mind," and, finishing his student's course in Christ's College, Cambridge, remained in that town, and exercised his ministry there for the rest of his life, not far really from Dry Drayton.

There was a class of people whom he pitied—the wild class, the rogues, vagabonds, criminals and prisoners. His wildness had not been of the same kind as theirs, but his course of folly and sin was worse in his eyes than theirs was. He pitied them; the country was full of them, and they had been increasing for generations—gypsies, rufflers (robbing market-women), prigmen (stealing clothes from hedges), upright men (the head villains of their companies), washmen (pretending to be lame), hookers (hauling clothes out of windows by means of long hooked sticks—even the very bedclothes off

1540	1550	1560	1570	1580	1590	1600	1610	1620
Henry	E	M	Elizabeth I				James I	
			Conversion ▶ Preacher in Cambridge					
			William Perkins					

the sleepers), and many others much worse. He persuaded
the gaoler at Cambridge to bring his great tribe of prisoners
to the "shierhouse" close to the prison. There he preached
to them while they sat and stood with fetters on their wrists,
and many of them were truly converted to God.

A remarkable instance was that of a condemned criminal.
Mr. Perkins, as was his custom, went with the prisoner to
the gallows. The young man went up the ladder and turned
round. He was supposed to speak to the people, but could
not; his head hung down and he looked pale and terrified.
"Are you afraid of death?" asked Mr. Perkins. "Ah no,"
said the man, "but of something worse." "Come down again
then," said he, "and see what God's grace will do to
strengthen you." When the poor fellow came down, he took
his hand and they both knelt. In prayer he spoke of all the
circumstances of the crime and of God's wrath against sin,
and of judgment and hell. The young man burst into tears
of anguish. (It used to be said by his hearers that when
Mr. Perkins pronounced the word "damn", it left a doleful
echo in their ears for a good while after, and that when he
spoke of the commandments, their hearts failed and their
hair almost stood upright.) But he then prayed that his sin
might be forgiven for the sake of the Lord Jesus Christ the
Saviour. He so spoke of the Lord's mercy and power to
deliver, of His faithfulness to His Son and His Word, and it
was so applied to the criminal's conscience, that it "made him
break out into new showres of tears of joie for the inward
consolation."

A crowd of people, as the young man mounted the ladder
with alacrity, saw him take his death as if he beheld heaven
opened. Some of them cried out, "Praise God! praise God!"

and when they reached home they spoke as if their journey that day had been not to the gallows but to Mount Tabor (where the Transfiguration is said to have been).

Mr. Perkins was a great reader. He got through books so quickly that he appeared to read nothing: and yet so accurately that he seemed to read everything. He used to write on the fly-leaf at the front of all his books, "Thou art a minister of the Word: mind thy business." Many of the books he wrote were translated into Latin, French, Dutch and Spanish, people thought so much of them. And he wrote them all left-handed, because he had something wrong with his right.

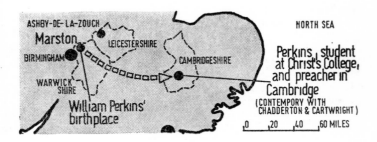

2. PERKINS' END AND COTTON'S BEGINNINGS

"Oft as the bell with solemn toll
Speaks the departure of a soul,
Let each one ask himself, 'Am I
Prepared, should I be called to die?' "

THE bell was tolling one day in the year 1602. It was the custom to ring it before death, while the grave, sad relations were watching round the deathbed, and the sick person was passing from this mortal life into the state that will never have an end. The great Mr. Perkins was dying—great, not in the opinion of worldly men, but in the hearts of godly men who had heard him preach in Cambridge.

1580	1590	1600	1610	1620	1630	1640	1650	1660
Elizabeth I		James I			Charles I		C OC	
William Perkins								Cromwell's
	Richard Sibbes							Letter
	JOHN COTTON (Preacher in America)							

Let us take a quiet peep into the room where he lies. He was in a good deal of pain, and a friend of his is praying to the Lord that the pain might be lessened. "Wait, wait" he says, "don't pray like that: but pray to the Lord to give me faith and patience, and then let Him lay on me whatever He pleases." Soon his spirit fled: he was only forty-four years old.

A student was walking through a field, and heard the passing bell, and, knowing that it must be for Mr. Perkins, felt very glad, and hoped he would really die soon. He died; and at the funeral a sermon was preached from the words: "Moses My servant is dead." There was a great concourse of people mourning because their friend and teacher was dead; yet still the student, John Cotton, felt secretly very glad. Why? Because Mr. Perkins' preaching had made him feel uneasy. He was clever and wanted to do well at the University, but after hearing the sermons he always had a feeling that if he began to trouble about religion, it would be a hindrance to him in his studies.

Time went on and Mr. Cotton became a Fellow and a Tutor. He enjoyed his work; it was stirring to see the students crowding in to his lectures, and flattering to overhear their praises, and he loved his work for its own sake too. But once, the remembrance of the passing-bell for Mr. Perkins came to his mind, and he seemed to see that in being glad because he need think no more about religion, he only showed himself to be a man who does not love God. Soon, the feeling seemed to be in his mind in all his leisure minutes. Once he went to hear Mr. Sibbes preach and after the service Mr. Cotton left the building feeling very heavy indeed. Here he was, he felt, all these years, with never a spark of God's grace, and actually having wanted to quench all thoughts of God and of eternal things, and his relief at Mr. Perkins' death was the heaviest part of the burden. The old writer of his Life says that God kept that burdened feeling upon his spirit. That was being convinced of sin; it was "the arrow of conviction." Mr. Cotton however did not know that. "Men see not the bright light that is in" that "cloud" when it overshadows them. "But thus he continued," the story says, "till it pleased God to let a word of faith into his heart, and to cause him to look unto Christ for his healing, which word also was dispensed unto him by the same Mr. Sibbes." And ever after there was a great love between these two good men.

JOHN COTTON
Vicar of Boston 1612-1633

It was on the very day of his marriage that he first obtained assurance of his interest in God's favour, which he never lost all his life. He used to say "The Lord made that day a day of double marriage."

He went as minister to Boston in Lincolnshire (do you know Boston Stump?) and after God had blessed his ministry there even the mayor and the majority of magistrates were called puritans. The best of men greatly loved him, and the worst of men greatly feared him.

A conceited, ignorant man once followed him home after sermon, and with frowns told him his preaching was become dark or flat. To whom he meekly answered, "Both, brother, it may be both: let me have your prayers that it may be otherwise."

On another occasion he was insulted by an impudent fellow in the street who called him an old fool: he replied, "I confess I am so. The Lord make thee and me wiser than we are, even wise unto salvation."

Eventually however he was persecuted for his nonconformist views, and left the country, first travelling to London in disguise.

After he reached America, and Boston was named after his first pastorate, he lived for years: in 1652 he had a letter written by Oliver Cromwell himself,

"Worthy sir, and my Christian friend,

I received yours a few dayes since. It was welcome to me because signed by you, whome I love and honour in the Lord . . .

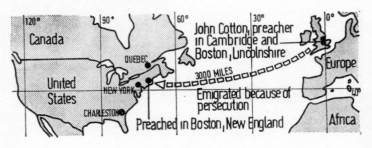

Surely, sir, the Lord is greatly to be feared as to be praised. Wee need your prayers in this as much as ever; how shall we behave ourselves after such mercyes? What is the Lord a doeinge? What prophesies are now fulfillinge? Who is a God like ours? To know his will, to doe his will, are both of him ...

I am a poor weake creature, and not worthye of the name of a worme; yet accepted to serve the Lord and his people. Indeed, my dear friend, between you and me, you knowe not me; my weaknesses, my inordinate passions, my unskill-fullnesse, and every way unfitnesse to my worke; yett the Lord, who will have mercye on whome he will, does as you see. Pray for me. Salute all Christian friendes, though unknown.

I rest your affectionate friend to serve you,

O. Cromwell."

And to finish with, here is a poem written by John Cotton, which shows you how thankful he felt to his Lord and God:

In mother's womb Thy fingers did me make,
And from the womb Thou didst me safely take:
From breast Thou hast me nursed my life throughout,
That I may say I never wanted ought.

In all my meals my table Thou hast spread;
In all my lodgings Thou hast made my bed;
Thou hast me clad with changes of array,
And changed my house for better far away.

In youthful wanderings Thou didst stay my slide;
In all my journeys Thou hast been my guide:
Thou hast me saved from many an unknown danger,
And showed me favour even where I was a stranger.

In both my callings Thou hast heard my voice;
In both my matches Thou hast made my choice;
Thou giv'st me sons and daughters, them to peer,
And giv'st me hope Thou'lt learn them Thee to fear.

Oft have I seen Thee look with mercy's face,
And through Thy Christ have felt Thy saving grace:
This is the heaven on earth, if any be:
For this, and all, my soul doth worship Thee.

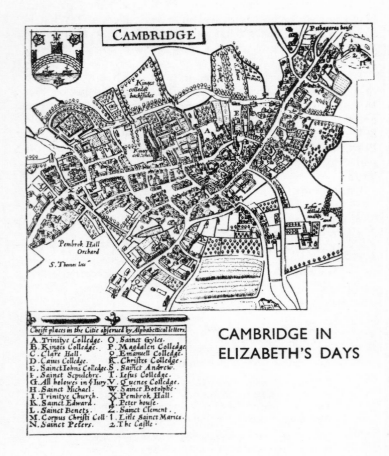

CAMBRIDGE

Kinges colledge backsydes

Knyes colledge

Pembrok Hall Orchard

S. Thomas lees

Pithagoras house

Cheist places in the Citie obserued by Alphabetical letters.

A. Trinitye Colledge.
B. Kinges Colledge.
C. Clare Hall.
D. Caius Colledge.
E. Sainct Iohns Colledge.
F. Sainct Sepulchre.
G. All holowes in ý Iury.
H. Sainct Michael.
I. Trinitye Church.
K. Sainct Edward.
L. Sainct Benets.
M. Corpus Christi Coll
N. Sainct Peters.

O. Sainct Gyles.
P. Magdalen Colledge.
Q. Emanuell Colledge.
R. Christes Colledge.
S. Sainct Andrew.
T. Iesus Colledge.
V. Quenes Colledge.
W. Sainct Botolph.
X. Pembrok Hall.
Y. Peter house.
Z. Sainct Clement.
1. Litle Sainct Maries.
2. The Castle.

CAMBRIDGE IN ELIZABETH'S DAYS

John Preston's Change

AMONGST the undergraduates in Queen's College, Cambridge, when a Mr. Oliver Bowles was a tutor, was John Preston. John's ancestors belonged to a family amongst the gentry in Lancashire; his great-grandfather had killed two men in duels, and fleeing into another country had lost much of his wealth, and now the Prestons were farmers. John had a high spirit and great ambition, and aimed for a place in the court of James I. So he associated at College with the young men whose fathers could easily gain Court positions for them, and entered into an arrangement to go to Paris to learn courtly ways. His uncle had left him a large sum of money and while it was in the keeping of a merchant to exchange for French money, the merchant died and the whole sum of money was lost. John was wild with disappointment and became sullen and gloomy over his blasted hopes. After a time his spirits rose, and he thought there was still hope for a Court life—he would be the best orator in College and gain a name; some duke who attended Court might engage him as a secretary; the king loved oratory and loved to have those about him who could argue. And now he was never seen away from his books, and took so little sleep that Mr. Bowles often told him that he ought to be more moderate or he would injure his health, and indeed when he was dying at the early age of 41, he knew that his neglected coughs at that time accounted for all his ill-health; for he even used to lay the bed-clothes over himself so that they would be sure to fall off at an early hour of the night and so the cold would wake him up.

While he was studying and looking forward to the future, he very much despised those who made the study of the Bible, and the Hebrew and Greek Testaments, and good

1580	1590	1600	1610	1620	1630	1640	1650	1660
Elizabeth I			James I		Charles I		C	O.C
	John Cotton		a sermon					
		John Preston	◄ Preached before James I					
		Oliver Bowles (tutor at Queen's College, Cambridge)						

books, their study; he thought it a most poor thing for a man to be a minister. There certainly was, he thought, one minister in Cambridge worth listening to—Mr. Cotton was an orator, and his addresses were full of Greek and Latin quotations. One day, with crowds of students from other colleges he went as before to hear Mr. Cotton. This was that John Cotton of whom I told you just now; the one who at first delighted in the students' applause, but who at length was taught by the Holy Spirit to leave enticing words of man's wisdom and to preach the gospel simply. This was the first time of Mr. Cotton's new preaching; the students were disappointed of the grand lecture they expected and Mr. Cotton saw it. He overheard no applauding remark after it, but noticed many a mutter and dark glance; their hopes had fallen flat. Mr. Cotton went to his room feeling, "Yes, it is so; I have lost their good will." He felt sad (for we like to be liked), but he thought: "Lord, I have counted the cost, let me count it loss for Thee." As he sat that evening someone knocked at the door; it was John Preston. God had spoken to him in that sermon making him feel that *one thing was needful*—not an appointment at Court, but the salvation of his soul; he had not known what to do or where to go after the sermon, but felt impelled to go to Mr. Cotton to ask him some anxious questions.

Shortly after that, not a duke only, but King James himself went to Cambridge, and those who could speak well had to take part in a debate before him. John Preston's part was an important one; it was the part of "first opponent"; he did his best as was his duty, and it was evident that His Majesty admired his speech more than the others, and that a way to Court was open before him if he was willing to take it. But all his feelings for Court life had died away, and the men who shortly before would have crowded round him with congratulations, when they saw that he did not follow up the matter, wondered at him. Why was it? could he too have begun to love people called "godly"? Was *he* too changed?

It was so indeed; he had passed from death unto life. In time he entered the ministry, the office he had once thought such a poor thing for a man, and he preached sometimes before the king and noblemen. "Why!" you may think, "I thought the story was about his being led away from great men." No; it is about his being taught not to *seek great things for himself,* and from the day of Mr. Cotton's sermon he never once sought them. He never had the gay grand life at Court he sought at first, but that did not mean that he ought to have worked on the farm at home. He had great grace and also great gifts, and he would have been like the servant who hid his talent in the earth (Matt. 25.25) if he had not used his gifts. The Lord said, "Blessed are the poor *in spirit;*" and Mr. Preston often felt poor and helpless when he had to preach before the great ones of the earth, and never sought great things for himself.

Once, when he was appointed to preach before the king, he was greatly helped, and delivered what he had prepared without notes. The king appeared very satisfied, and commented that Preston had made it very clear that the

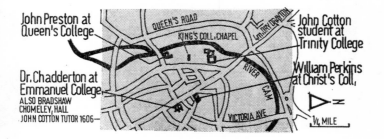

John Preston at Queen's College

QUEEN'S ROAD

KING'S COLL. CHAPEL

John Cotton student at Trinity College

Dr. Chadderton at Emmanuel College

ALSO BRADSHAW
CHOMELEY, HALL
JOHN COTTON TUTOR 1606

RIVER CAM

VICTORIA AVE

William Perkins at Christ's Coll.

¼ MILE

Arminians put God in the same difficulty as Darius was in when he wanted to save Daniel but could not.

JOHN PRESTON

John Preston's Friend

I have already said that John Preston pleased the king by his ability to make a good speech, and that he might easily have got a place at Court if he had tried but that he did not try; and some of his college friends began to dislike him because they were afraid that he had begun to think about his never-dying soul and eternity. As time went on they grew more sure than ever that he was 'turning Puritan', especially after one particular incident which I will now tell you.

In those days boys went to college much earlier than they do now, and many of the students were in their early teens only. Mr. Preston was now a tutor in the college, and he had one young Morgan, an orphan. The Morgan family belonged to Mr. Preston's native place; they were very rich and the Prestons were "decayed", and they had often helped them—not with food and clothing (they had them), but with large helps, such as a whole farm! So the Prestons were grateful to the Morgans, and when the orphan boy was sent by his uncles to be under Mr. Preston's tuition at College, he felt that he must be like a good kind elder brother to him; and not teach him only, but care for him, advise him and help him. Some of Morgan's friends were Papists (Roman Catholics), and his uncles though not very religious men, did not want him to become a Papist; and so they chose to send him to Mr. Preston at Cambridge rather than to Oxford; Cambridge was more Protestant than Oxford.

Now King James I liked visiting the University; he had very much enjoyed the debate at Cambridge of which I told you and he sent word that he would come again. The heads of the colleges determined that this time the students should act a play before him; it was called "Ignoramus," and was written nearly all in Latin, but some of it was bad Latin such as an "ignoramus" would use. They knew that King James would laugh at it (and he did) because he was very proud of his own correct Latin. Young Morgan was very good-looking, and it was suggested that the part of a lady in the play should be taken by him. When a boy was fixed upon to act his tutor was asked for his consent, and some of the tutors were only too proud that a pupil of theirs should act before the king. But Mr. Preston felt that he could not give his consent and a letter was sent to Morgan's guardians about it. They thought "Mr. Preston is too precise; this might be a step to promotion for our nephew;" and allowed him to take the part. And not only so but they removed him from Mr. Preston's care altogether, and sent him to Oxford, and there he became very independent, went in for pleasure more than for study, and at last actually became a Papist also, and brought grief and trouble to his relatives.

Now while it was not easy at the time for Mr. Preston to forego the favour of the Morgan family in that way, his decision about the play was strengthening to some others, and especially to his friend Samuel Fairclough, a young man of twenty, and eight years younger than himself. Fairclough had not then taken all his examinations; he was an excellent Latin scholar and very much in favour with the principals because of his promising 'parts' and his nice bearing towards themselves. He had a plump genial face and was short, and someone proposed that he was just the one for the part of Surda, an old woman in the play. But what were his own thoughts when he was told, "Fairclough, you're put down

John Preston tutor at Queen's college. Samuel Fairclough student

QUEEN'S ROAD
KING'S COLLEGE CHAPEL

Fairclough later declined mastership of Trinity college.

Richard Blacker by at Trinity college (SEE LATER ACCOUNT)

VICTORIA AVE.

¼ MILE

1590	1600	1610	1620	1630	1640	1650	1660	1670
Elizabeth I	James I			Charles I		C	O.C	Charles II
John Preston								
The play	Samuel Fairclough							

for Surda"? simply, that he must not be in the play at all. He was not a pupil of Mr. Preston's, and indeed it was not until afterwards that Mr. Preston heard about his refusal. Samuel went to the Vice-Chancellor himself and asked that he might be excused from that part and from any other. "Oh, but Fairclough," said the Vice-Chancellor, "that is unwise; if you act well now, you may get preferment at court in a short time, the King has such a keen ear for good speakers." "But," said Fairclough, "I would have to wear woman's clothes, and that is not right." The Vice-Chancellor laughed with a hearty laugh, saying it was only a play, he was not deceiving people by pretending to *be* a woman. But Samuel thought that did not matter, the Bible says "The woman shall not wear that which pertaineth unto a man, neither shall a man put on a woman's garment, for all that do so are abomination unto the Lord" (Deut. 22.5), and he could not feel it was pleasing to the Lord even although everybody knew it was only pretence. But the Vice-Chancellor looked upon the play as a very clever hit at some lawyers who deserved to be hit; oh a splendid piece! And besides, Surda's part was only in three little scenes out of fifty—three, and not many sentences at that! Should he give way? Was it absurd to keep out of it? Was there not in any part of the play some bad or flippant little thing or some half-swearing word? Yes, there was. So what Samuel asked was to be excused from taking *any* part in it, and the Vice Chancellor's laugh turned to a dark impatient frown, and Samuel went out of the room no longer "in favour and tender love" with him. "This," said the Vice Chancellor, "will have to go higher." Who likes to hear that—"This must go higher"?

Who would be told? Might it even be called despising the King? Before it went higher however, someone who was taking another part said, "Let me play Surda too," and took it; and there it ended, but Samuel knew that it was God who had not let it go 'higher.' He rules the raging of the sea and says, "Hitherto shalt thou go and no further;" and He often says "Thou shalt not be given into the hand of the men of whom thou art afraid." (Jer. 39.17).

Finally, I must first finish telling you how useful Mr. Preston ended his life. He was only forty-one, but he said, "The important question is not *how long* I have lived, but *how* I have lived." As he lay dying on that particular Lord's Day in July, he said, "Let me go to my home, and to Jesus Christ who has bought me with His precious blood . . . I feel death coming to my heart. My pain shall now be turned into joy."

Poor Mr. Bains

IN the 1600s some of the most godly ministers in England would preach to their people year after year, and then suddenly an order would come to them to go and see the Bishop. When they saw him he would question them, and then often end by telling them not to preach any more, nor dare to go into their pulpit again; and indeed he would leave them no choice but quite prevent them from doing so. The reason generally was that the bishop liked to have the church 'high,' and the minister did not; he liked to have everything in his church very plain, or 'pure'. Because of that he was called a Puritan.

It was not every bishop who was hard on the Puritan ministers; some were good and gentle. And it was not all the "plain" ministers who were good and godly preachers, but a great many of them were, and certainly poor Mr. Bains was.

In one way we ought not to say 'Poor Mr. Bains,' any more than we should 'poor John' or 'poor Paul' meaning the apostle John or the apostle Paul. John and Paul were holy men of God, and they did not grumble because of what they suffered, and neither did Paul Bains (for his name was Paul too). He was not an apostle, but an English Puritan. But he had such a heavenly majesty in his face sometimes that it gave people a feeling of awe to look at him. He prayed to God a very great deal and felt that God was speaking to him, and it was that that gave such a look to his countenance.

Once he had been far from God; when he was young, he grieved his father so much with his wild ways that he thought, "I cannot leave all this money to Paul, he would squander it." So he said to a very upright young man whom he knew, "Mr. Wilson, I leave this money with you; if my poor son ever leaves off his wicked ways, let him have it."

Paul knew nothing of that, but God who had chosen him long before he was born, made him forsake those wicked ways, and when Mr. Wilson found him to be a godly young man, he gave him the money.

Mr. Wilson lay dying himself, soon after that, and he said, "Oh, Paul! do be a friend to my wife and two children." So Mr. Bains *was* a friend to them; in fact he married the poor widow and did all he could for the children.

Now in Cambridge there had been a great and good man—yes, you know!—Mr. Perkins. Many people had been converted by hearing him preach. After he died Mr. Bains was the next minister to fill his pulpit. Mr. Bains's sermons were solemn, and while he preached God spoke to the heart of another of His chosen ones, Richard Sibbes, who followed the footsteps of both these good men, and was indeed, the most blessed of the three.

A godly gentleman placed his son under Mr. Bains, and one evening while Mr. Bains was having some friends for supper, he sent this lad into town for something they wanted. He didn't come back as soon as he expected, so when he did arrive he told him off in no uncertain terms: the boy was silent. But the next day, when Mr. Bains was calm again, he said "My father placed me under your care not only to learn, but also because of your example in how to live in the fear of God. But, sir, you have given me a very *bad* example such as I never saw even in my father's house." "Oh" said Mr. Bains suddenly overwhelmed with sorrow. "Go to my tailor and order yourself a new suit, and I'll pay to show

Sibbes studied at St. John's college, Master at St. Catherine's, Curate, Holy Trinity ch,

Perkins then Bains lecturers, St. Andrew's ch, Perkins fellow & Bains at Christ's college

'He told him off in no uncertain terms'

how sorry I am." And always after that he was much quieter and thoughtful about the way he spoke. For some years he went on with his useful work.

But while Mr. Bains was thus leading the life of a quiet, holy minister, three things happened to him almost at once— his wife died, he lost his health and strength, and the bishop suddenly said, "Leave your church, leave your people"!

And so he was a *"silenced"* minister. Somebody took the two children—perhaps their Aunt Sheafe who lived in Cranbrook—but poor Mr. Bains never had a real home after that. He was always short of money and for the greater part of the year he would lodge where he could, in poverty and want. It was when I read and thought of his having no place at all to call 'home' that I thought, 'Poor Mr. Bains.'

Yet with the summer, sunshine often came to the lonely prophet in this way. One rich gentleman or another would ask him to spend a few weeks under his roof, and during

1560	1570	1580	1590	1600	1610	1620	1630	1640

Elizabeth I   James I   Charles I

William Perkins Cambridge pulpit

Paul Bains

Richard Sibbes

those weeks the news would spread that he was there. It was a time when numbers of people had great conflicts in their souls and could not rest; the Spirit of God convinced them of sin very powerfully indeed; often ministers were visited by these awakened distressed ones, and Mr. Bains had many such to visit him.

Now the bishop heard of this. "What!" he said, "I silenced him in Cambridge, and here he is, keeping a conventicle in a house!" and at once he summoned him before the council. It was the dreadful "Court of High Commission," and sometimes good men went to prison from that court.

Yet that evening, or the next day, there was Mr. Bains riding along on horseback to his friend's house again! What a happy day that was; he was quite free, and he never had any more trouble of that kind. What had happened was this: there were some bishops and noblemen sitting at the table, and when the accusation against Mr. Bains was read out, one nobleman said, "Speak; speak for yourself." Mr. Bains at once made such a speech that another of the noblemen at the table sprang up and said, "He speaks more like an angel than a man, and I dare not stay here to have a hand in any sentence against him." And indeed a *fear* seemed to be upon the Court and Mr. Bains was dismissed.

Richard Blackerby

YOU remember me telling you about Samuel Fairclough who would not join in a play and act the part of a woman? Well, when Samuel was quite grown up he became a minister, but while he was still a young man he passed a year or two in the house and school of a Mr. Richard Blackerby, and this chapter is about him.

The first time we read about Richard Blackerby takes us back to the days of Queen Elizabeth, when he too was a student in Cambridge. He attended the ministry of famous Mr. Perkins and through his preaching was born again of the Holy Spirit. For some years he was in perplexity and distress of soul, and his father, thinking Cambridge surely did not suit his health, took him home and hoped that his sadness would pass away. But it did not pass away, and at last he gained his father's permission to go back to Cambridge. "And it pleased God," the account of three hundred years ago says, "as he was returning to Cambridge and riding alone upon Newmarket Heath, bemoaning his sad condition before the Lord, to reveal His reconciled face in Christ Jesus to him."

Mr. Blackerby preached in Norfolk and Suffolk for some years, but being 'silenced' went and preached in Essex and Cambridgeshire, and God sent such power with his preaching that great numbers of people were converted. His name is quite forgotten now, compared with the names of many godly men who lived long ago, such as John Bunyan; but Mr. Blackerby did not write books, he was raised up for his own day, and it was said that two thousand people were called by grace under his ministry. It was said he never lost a moment in idleness. He rose early, winter and summer, and spent the whole of each day reading, meditating, in prayer and in teaching others. He once preached at Castle Hedingham

1570	1580	1590	1600	1610	1620	1630	1640	1650
Elizabeth I				James I		Charles I		C
William Perkins' preaching								
RICHARD BLACKERBY								
			Samuel Fairclough					▶

where some young people had a dancing club; when the news spread that grave Blackerby was going to preach, they thought: "Anything for sport, we will go." You may have heard how people used to mock the Puritans, and in some storybooks great fun is made of the long faces some of them put on, the whining tones in which they spoke, and the ridiculous names they gave their children,—names like "Fly-debate" Roberts. Satan has many wiles or tricks, and one of them is to bring God's work and people into contempt, and he did that in the days of the Puritans by sending many hypocrites into their ranks. Perhaps these young men and girls thought they would find some such things to amuse them in Mr. Blackerby, but it was not so. They were nearly all converted by means of his sermon, and from that time they turned the club into a prayer-meeting. Mr. Blackerby was grave, but not 'long-faced'; he did not put on a voice, thinking, "Now this voice will sound holy"; and he certainly did not call his child 'Fly-debate'.

Nobody is quite free from all hypocrisy, but in those days God did a very mighty work in England in bringing many thousands of His elect people into a state of grace, and Satan tried one of his mightiest works too. The chief hypocrites were Jesuits, who purposely pretended to be Puritans, and wore long faces and made long prayers to stir up dislike and ridicule.

Mr. Blackerby's prayers were short and frequent, and his expression was generally cheerful and gentle. One rule in his household was a rule which I think would never have been made by one of those veiled-Jesuit Puritan ministers; it was, that after dinner on the Lord's day all those who could should have a nap, especially those who were apt to sleep during service-time, lest they should profane God's worship by sleeping in the congregation. That long sour face was the best that Satan, the Jesuits, or any bad men, could do, in imitation of a certain expression possessed by not a few of God's servants; but it was a miserable sham; they could not get into their eyes that majestic gravity (Mr. Blackerby was noted for it) that often struck terror into evil-doers. It was said that when he preached his hearers either fell graciously under the power of his ministry, or kicked violently against it.

Matters were intensely real to him, and he felt his own sins deeply, although they used to say he was one of the holiest men living. He told one of his grandchildren, "Oh, you little think what a vile heart I have, and how I am plagued with proud thoughts. Child, if you know God, pray for me that He would purify this filthy heart. If God did not enable me to watch over it in some measure, I should act shamefully." He used to say the same as Mr. Perkins, "If a man is once acquainted with his own heart, he will be apt to think everyone better than himself; and if the love of God appears in any man, it will make him put the best construction possible on other people's words and actions."

When his eldest daughter, whom he loved very much, died, he preached the funeral sermon saying he believed she feared God from three years old. He preached as one who had not lost his God though he had lost his dearest child.

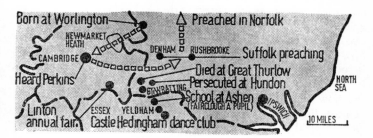

Born at Worlington — Preached in Norfolk
NEWMARKET HEATH
CAMBRIDGE DENHAM RUSHBROOKE Suffolk preaching
Heard Perkins Died at Great Thurlow
Persecuted at Hundon NORTH SEA
STAMBRUTING School at Ashen
(FAIRCLOUGH A PUPIL) IPSWICH
Linton ESSEX YELDHAM
annual fair Castle Hedingham dance club 10 MILES

The love of the created one could never draw his heart away from the Creator.

Once he preached at Linton, where the annual fair had been held on the Sabbath ever since popish times, but never again on that holy day. When he preached at Hundon, some of the worldly people of the place did not rest till they got rid of him; they did not like to hear about death, hell and judgment, and did not want the water of life; so they got up some little excuse to tell the bishop—it may have been that Mr. Blackerby did not put a surplice on. It was then that the bishop silenced him. Out in the churchyard one man said, "Now we're rid of old Blackerby, he won't preach here again;" and a woman hearing him, spoke very solemnly to him telling him that Mr. Blackerby would preach there again when he was dead. That very day eight years after, that man was buried, and the Lord's day after, Mr. Blackerby had liberty to preach again in Suffolk, and preached in Hundon pulpit.

Mr. Blackerby's school was in Ashen, a village in Essex. Samuel Fairclough and his friend Christopher Burrell went, not to teach, but to perfect themselves in Hebrew and Greek under Mr. Blackerby's tuition, for he was a great Hebrew scholar. Mr. Fairclough married his elder daughter and Mr. Burrell his younger.

When he was preaching, he wanted most of all to show what the scripture meant, and then to show how it applied to his hearers. He closely studied the Hebrew and Greek, in which languages the Bible was originally written, and spent much time in holy converse with God. He had reason to believe that God had made him the spiritual father of over two thousand persons. The word of God coming from his lips, it had the same effect as when the apostles preached— it soon became the savour of life unto life to those that heard it, or they became enraged against it; and sad it was to see how God's judgments fell on some of those who raged against his preaching. But others could say, "His reproofs were dipped in oil, driven into the heart, and received with all acceptation, because of the overcoming kindness with which they were attended."

Once he was with some wealthy people who swore and used profane language. He left their company, looking sad, yet when he had them on their own, he spoke to them lovingly and seriously; one gentlemen on such an occasion, said, "If you had reproved me at the table, I would have stabbed you; but now I thank you."

Getting ready for the Lord's day, he usually preached in his own house on the Saturday afternoon to get ready; and on the day of rest he prayed six times with his family as well as expounding the scriptures.

When the persecuting bishops were laid aside, Mr. Blackerby could be a minister in a church again, without having to perform any of those ceremonies that had offended his conscience so; and in this way he was chosen pastor of Great Thurlow in Suffolk, where he spent the rest of his life.

One afternoon when in his old age he was living in Mr. Burrell's house in Great Wratting, he set out to visit a person who was in great trouble of soul. When he was younger he used to ride on horseback, visiting the sick in Ashen, Yeldham, and places near. That afternoon however, he went on foot and his Daughter Burrell was with him. Their way lay through a field where there was a bull that used to do a

'The bull stopped, and roaring, turned right away'

great deal of harm. When it saw them it made for them in mad fury, and when it was very near Mr. Blackerby put off his hat and prayed, "Lord, if our way be of Thee, stay the fury of this beast;" and immediately the bull stopped, and roaring turned right away.

He often said before he died that for more than forty years he never had a single doubt of his salvation—what a favour this was! At length, he was taken ill in his pulpit, and they carried him home, where he remained for six weeks, and then passed away in 1648. He was a good man: Mr. Daniel Rogers of Wethersfield, another loved minister, used to say he could never come into Mr. Blackerby's presence without trembling. And so it was, if I read Isaiah 66.5 aright, with Mr. Blackerby himself before God, and the Lord appeared to his everlasting joy.

Sir Nathaniel and November 5th

IN the time of the Puritans, somebody who knew the county of Suffolk very well called Sir Nathaniel Barnardiston "the top branch of the Suffolk cedars." He was Lord of the Manor of Kedington, and the twenty-third in succession of a family who had had the estate from the time of the Norman Conquest. Suffolk was rich in "trees of righteousness" in puritan times, low trees and high trees, privet bushes and cedars, and the unknown one who gave this title to Sir Nathaniel must have esteemed him very highly in love.

Sir Nathaniel knew the Lord from his early days. Two verses of the Bible and the sermons preached from them, had brought life to him. One was "Behold, I was shapen in iniquity, and in sin did my mother conceive me" (Psa. 51.5); and the other, "This is His commandment, That we should believe on the name of His Son Jesus Christ" (1 John 3.23). When he grew up he went about with a pleasant yet grave look. He was a magistrate, and sometimes his grave look struck awe into the prisoner before him. In the year 1624 he was made sheriff of the whole county of Suffolk, and during that year he used to take his sheriffs-men with him every week to hear a week-night sermon in Clare. He was constantly chosen as Member of Parliament as his fore-fathers had been, and they said the country rang with the cry, "A Barnardiston! a Barnardiston!"

It was not all pleasure in the reign of Charles I to be a magistrate, a sheriff, or an M.P. Sir Nathaniel suffered imprisonment for a long time for fighting the same battle that Hampden fought—struggling against unlawful taxing, such as the notorious ship-money, about which you learn in your history books.

1590	1600	1610	1620	1630	1640	1650	1660	1670
Elizabeth I	James I			Charles I		C	O.C.	Charles II

Sir Nathaniel Barnardiston

gunpowder plot ▬   prison ▲ ministry at Kedington ▼

Samuel Fairclough

He had a great veneration for his godly father and grand-father. Their family tree had brought forth buds and blossoms after the wintry ages of Popery, and he was at least the third to share the blessings of the Reformation. His grandfather had been sent to Geneva in Queen Mary's reign to be educa-ted by John Calvin himself. Sir Nathaniel looked upon God's goodness in mercies and providences to people's ancestors, as a binding obligation to themselves to give thanks and praise to Him. He had grace not to think: "Is not this great Kedington or great Barnardiston that I have builded?" not that these sweet little spots are great, they are small; and yet there was something in a country manor, very rich in the good things of earth. Sir Nathaniel had a keen consciousness that they were passing things only, and used to say he would rather see one grain of grace in his children than that their lands had been a hundred times more extensive than they were. The names of the children were Thomas, Nathaniel, Samuel, Stephen, John, Peletia, William, Arthur, Ann and Jane—all simple English names, except Peletia; no grotesque names like Fly-Debate, the name I mentioned before.

At one time there were ten or more servants in the family who were God-fearing people. After every meal they sang a psalm before rising from table in the servants' hall. The head servant usually, after every sermon they heard, called the rest into the buttery to repeat it to them before they were all called into the library to repeat it to their master. The repetition was not word for word, though the custom was called "repeating the sermon"; but in those days children and servants were gathered together to answer questions put by their father and master, or repeat portions as he chose. Sir Nathaniel's head-servant had a good example in the Bible,—the faithful servant who prayed, "O God of my master Abraham;" and God's blessing on England was so rich in those days that there were many Abrahams like Sir Nathaniel, and many servants like Eliezer. Things had changed for the better.

It fell to Sir Nathaniel to say who was to be the minister. Nothing made him pray more earnestly, and the one whom he chose for Kedington was Mr. Samuel Fairclough. Several years had passed since Mr. F. had been with Mr. Blackerby at Ashen, and there is much more to tell about him, right from when he was a boy.

Years before, on a lovely day in late summer, two school-boys, this Samuel Fairclough and John Trigg, went down to an orchard in the old town of Haverhill where they lived, because they knew of some splendid ripe pears that were just right for eating. They took good care to wait till no-one was about, and then they ate as many as they could, and last of all stuffed their pockets full of the delicious pears.

But oh! the next Sunday when Samuel was listening to the sermon, what should the minister speak about but Zaccheus, and how the Lord called him out of the tree, and how the Lord's mercy and lovingkindness to him made him promise to restore all that he had wrongly taken from any-one. The minister repeated with emphasis that no man can expect pardon from God for wrong done to someone else

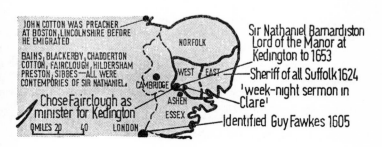

JOHN COTTON WAS PREACHER AT BOSTON, LINCOLNSHIRE BEFORE HE EMIGRATED

BAINS, BLACKERBY, CHADDERTON, COTTON, FAIRCLOUGH, HILDERSHAM, PRESTON, SIBBES—ALL WERE CONTEMPORIES OF SIR NATHANIEL.

Chose Fairclough as minister for Kedington

0 MILES 20   40   LONDON

NORFOLK

WEST / EAST

CAMBRIDGE

ASHEN

ESSEX

Sir Nathaniel Barnardiston Lord of the Manor at Kedington to 1653

Sheriff of all Suffolk 1624

'week-night sermon in Clare'

Identified Guy Fawkes 1605

unless he makes full restitution to the person if at all possible. You can imagine what Samuel felt, sitting there; the memory of all those pears. Money was worth a lot in those days, and Samuel didn't see much of it, but he knew those pears must have been worth three precious pence.

Samuel couldn't get any sleep that night; and getting up early Monday morning he went to his friend John, and told him he was going to the owner of the orchard, Goodman Jude, to pay him twelve pence. Poor John thought the owner of the orchard, instead of forgiving, would tell the schoolmaster, and he knew what would happen then!—but though John tried to put him off, Samuel wouldn't listen. "Look, Sam," said John, "you talk like a fool; God will forgive us ten times sooner than old Jude will forgive us once." But off went Sam just the same, and told Jude why he had come, and offered him his shilling. The old man to Sam's surprise readily forgave him, and wouldn't even accept the shilling! Now what was he to do? It wasn't until he had gone to his minister to tell him everything, that it wasn't just the stolen pears but sin in his heart and all through his life that was troubling him, that through the minister's kind words of pardon through Jesus Christ, Samuel's heart was quiet—he was at peace with God. All his questions were answered, and God's grace to him proved real. How thankful the minister was—he was only in his early twenties himself; you can imagine how he rejoiced to see Samuel become a good servant of Jesus Christ, much used by God in bringing souls to know the same pardoning love that had meant so much to him. And so Samuel Fairclough became the minister of Kedington in Suffolk. His boyhood friend John Trigg later became a physician in London; I wonder how often *he* remembered the stolen pears.

The minister who preached about Zaccheus was named Samuel Ward, and when he was 26 he moved to be the preacher at Ipswich for many years. But now we must return to our story about Samuel Fairclough.

One particular day, year after year, he and Sir Nathaniel spent together, was November 5th. It was not only when

the damp afternoon faded into darkness that the people began
to remember the 5th of November. We must picture the
whole family and servants and the whole village first listening
to Mr. Fairclough preaching in the morning about God's
great mercy in delivering England from popery. And before
he preached he had to read a long proclamation from
Parliament, one sentence of which was that "*thankfulness*
might *never be forgotten,* and that all ages to come might
yield praise to God for THIS JOYFUL DAY OF DELIVERANCE."

At dinner-time there was a great feast at the Manor House
for friends and neighbours, a great feast in the servants' hall
for their friends, and an extra special feast and gifts of food
and clothing for the poor. Before they all went out to light
the bonfire the Squire made a speech, as many masters did.
But there was one part the children always liked to hear,
and that was when Sir Nathaniel told them that in 1605, when
he was seventeen years old, he was one afternoon in Temple
Gardens, and noticed several men walking there together and
constantly whispering. And all these men in a few days, he
found to be Guy Fawkes and the very conspirators of the
Gunpowder Plot, for he went to "view" them in the prison!
Yes, a *hand* had been laid on Guy's shoulder, *just in time.*

I think perhaps they too knew and sang some of the psalms
put into metre by William Whittingham; perhaps the 121st
just suited such an occasion—

> I lift my eyes to Sion hill,
>   From whence I do attend,
>   Till succour God me send:
> The mighty God me succour will,
>   Which heaven and earth did frame,
>   And all things therein name.
>
> Thy foot from slip he will preserve,
>   And will thee safely keep;
>   For he doth never sleep:
> Lo, he that Israel doth conserve,
>   Sleep never can surprise,
>   Nor slumber close his eyes.
>
> The Lord thy keeper is alway,
>   On thy right hand is he
>   A shade to cover thee:

The sun shall not thee parch by day,
　　Nor moon, scarce half so bright,
　　With cold thee hurt by night.

The Lord will keep thee from distress,
　　And will thy life sure save:
　　Yea, thou shalt also have
In all thy business good success;
　　When thou go'st in or out
　　He'll compass thee about.

Or it might have been the 127th, for in these days they sang only the psalms:

Except the Lord the house doth make,
　　And thereunto doth set his hand,
　　What men do build, it cannot stand;
Likewise in vain men undertake
Cities and holds to watch and ward,
Except the Lord be their safeguard.

Though in the morn ye rise early,
　　And so at night go late to bed,
　　Eating with carefulness your bread,
Your labour is but vanity:
But they whom God doth love and keep,
Enjoy all things with quiet sleep.

Therefore mark well when ye do see
　　That men have hearts t'enjoy their land,
　　It is the gift of God's own hand:
For God doth multiply to thee
Of his great liberality,
The blessing of posterity.

And when the children come to age,
　　They grow in strength and activeness,
　　In person and in comeliness:
So that a shaft shot with courage
Of one that hath a most strong arm,
Flies not so swift, nor doth like harm.

Oh, well is he that hath his quiver
　　Furnished with such artillery:
　　For when in peril he shall be,
Such one shall never quake or shiver,
When he doth plead before the judge
Against his foes that bear him grudge.

And how well Mr. Fairclough proved these words true we must leave till the next chapter.

Mr. Fairclough's Lambs

THERE was a deep pond in one of the Kedington fields that was a danger. "A pond! why? surely anyone with sense might see where he was going!" Yes, but he might be as sensible and careful as anyone else, and yet be absent-minded only once for a few minutes, and it might be just then that he did *not* see where he was going. "Safety is of the Lord" (Prov. 21.31), and so is deliverance; so are guidance in prayer and answers to prayer and Mr. and Mrs. Fairclough found it so on one memorable occasion.

Mrs. Fairclough was so frail and delicate, that it almost seemed as if death might soon part the husband and wife— that if a fever came along Mrs. Fairclough would be sure to die. Mr. Fairclough felt anxious about her, and one day he scarcely did anything but kneel down and pray for her. He did so again and again, and in the evening, instead of feeling tired of offering up the same petitions, he felt that God was near and heard him. He was on his knees for the seventh time when he heard a shriek. It was the voice of his wife. He ran to the pond, caught her by the hand and pulled her out just before she was about to sink for the third time. It was an October evening, and she had gone for a little twilight walk by herself to be in the open air, and (as her custom was) to meditate in the field on the promises of God, before lighting candles and taking up her sewing for the evening. She had not noticed where she was walking. The water was cold, and yet no pneumonia, no fever, followed, and indeed it was not long before she became perfectly well and strong.

The usual time for Mr. Fairclough to go for a walk was Saturday afternoon. He would go through the quiet fields and pray. On these occasions he very often found himself praying for his friends and relations, and one Saturday about

'He caught her by the hand'

four o'clock, he felt as if he must pray fervently for his youngest little boy who was two years old. For half-an-hour his mind was wholly taken up with asking the Lord to bless, preserve and teach him. When he returned home it was to hear a wonderful story:—the little boy had fallen from the attic window to the ground! Beside the back door there was a deep barrel of water with ducklings swimming about it, and a quarter of a yard away from the barrel lay a heavy old door with duck's food on it. The little boy fell between the barrel and the old door, and while broken tiles from the eaves of the second storey (which he had struck in his fall) lay all round, not one touched him. He was picked up unconscious, but in a short time he opened his eyes, and before his father reached home was running about as though nothing had happened. Father, mother, brothers, sisters, and the careless servant (who, at four o'clock had taken him up to the

1600	1610	1620	1630	1640	1650	1660	1670	1680
E₁	James I		Charles I		C	OC	Charles II	
stole pears				Minister at Kedington, Suffolk				
SAMUEL FAIRCLOUGH								

attic and had let him lean far out of the window by himself)
could not understand how he had escaped death. Mr. Fairclough sent for many of the neighbours to join him in
thanking God.

Another time their baby, a little girl six months old began
to lose all her brightness. She would often moan and cry,
but worse than that she often uttered piercing screams, and
even the doctor could not find out the cause. After some
weeks Mr. Fairclough set apart a day for the whole family
to fast and pray, and once more he felt that his prayers were
heard. The next day Mrs. Fairclough was stroking her baby's
head when she felt a pin prick her hand, and looking closely
into its ear noticed the tip of a pin. With great difficulty she
got it out. It was a big pin and rusty, and the poor little
child being set at rest was soon well.

These answers to his prayers for his little ones made Mr.
Fairclough profoundly thankful and in his thankfulness he
vowed a vow; each time he vowed, and ever after kept his
vow. A vow is a promise made to God. The Bible says,
"When thou vowest a vow unto God, defer not to pay it;
for He hath no pleasure in fools: pay that which thou hast
vowed. Better is it that thou shouldest not vow, than that
thou shouldest vow and not pay" (Eccles. 5. 4,5). A vow is a
solemn thing, but Mr. Fairclough felt that it was his solemn
duty to show his thankfulness to God by some act such as
some special kindness to the poor. His stipend was paid
to him partly in money and partly in useful things—an old-
fashioned custom which is no longer observed. Wool ready
to be made into cloth, or ready to be used as knitting, was
one thing he received. The day after his little boy fell down
he made and signed a solemn promise before all the con-

gregation that as long as he lived in Kedington, he would give all the wool to the poor. When the prayer for his baby was granted he made a similar vow. On that occasion, it was that he would give all the lambs (for he received lambs which fed in his own meadow) to the poor; if there were any of his poor people who could not benefit by having a lamb or two given to them, he promised to give them the value of them in money.

It was a most interesting thing for all the people to hear him announce after the evening service, "Brethren, after due consideration of the lawfulness of making vows in some cases, and after a humble acknowledgment of my own weakness and unworthiness, I have invocated the grace of God both for strength to enable me to perform this ... and for Divine favour in accepting me in it through the merits of Jesus Christ. I do solemnly vow and covenant with God, and expressly promise unto you ... that I will give the wool ..." etc.

For thirty-five years Mr. Fairclough lived in Kedington. He had seven children to bring up and not much money, but to the end the poor had the wool and the full value of the lambs. He also thought of the old people whose sight was not so good as it used to be, and provided them with large-print Bibles, and spectacles to go with them.

Once when he was thanked for a sermon, he replied, "Give God the glory! no praise was due to the rams' horns when the walls of Jericho fell." So you see how useful he was all his life long, and 'after he had served his own generation by the will of God, fell on sleep.'

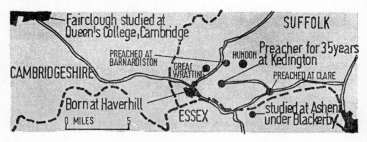

Sir Samuel's Letters

SIR Samuel Barnardiston, of Bishopsgate Street, London, was the son of good Sir Nathaniel, whom I told you about, the Suffolk Squire who made Guy Fawkes Day such a happy day for the children. Those days were a far-away memory to Sir Samuel, as he sat writing his letters in November 1683.

He had taught *his* children that "The Gunpowder Plot should never be forgot"; but they were then living in such dreadful times that it seemed as if it would be forgotten very soon. The King was a secret papist; his brother who would be King after him was an open papist, and if popery was established by law all happy freedom would be at an end, and all right religion would be crushed. Indeed, it was being crushed more and more as time went on, and Sir Samuel took it very much to heart. When he wrote his letters he would every now and then break off from the private parts—such as, "I hope our dear friend Mr. Wright is better" —and write something about the sad happenings at Court or in Parliament. And if any of the public news was a little brighter, he would put that too.

In the summer of that year, Lord William Russell was most unjustly put to death. He had been one of the greatest patriots and most outspoken Protestants in the Kingdom. Another as patriotic, Algernon Sidney, was in the Tower sentenced to death, but reprieved for a while, in November 1683. During those few brighter weeks, Sir Samuel would fill a good part of the letter with the happy news of the reprieve. Living in London, he was able to give his old friends in Suffolk very true accounts of what went on. Sir Samuel was a man of influence and had much to attend to, and used to write his letters out roughly, get his secretary to make a neat copy of each, then choose whether he would

1620	1630	1640	1650	1660	1670	1680	1690	1700
J	Charles I			C	O.C	Charles II		J.	W+M	Anne

| Sir Nathaniel Barnardiston | | | | | fine & prison | |

| Sir Samuel Barnardiston | | | | | | |

| | | | | 'Judge Jefferys' | | died in Tower |

keep his own or the secretary's copy, have them addressed,
and then placed in a window-sill, and one of the boy servants
would come and take them to the post-house.

But alas! Sir Samuel's secretary, Nehemiah Osland, was a
traitor to his master. The few bright weeks of Sidney's
reprieve passed, and he was brought to the block after all:
and the cry again was, "Up with the King's High Church
party! Up with the Duke's popish party! down with the sour,
gloomy Protestant party! root them out!" Osland thought:
Why! I would get money if I showed these letters to the
court: they would thank me if I made out that anybody
who was capable of praising Lord Russell might start a
Protestant plot some day. And so he showed them, and had
his money, and Sir Samuel was imprisoned in a house, and
told that in February he was to be convicted of "High Misdemeanour" (that is, very bad behaviour, almost crime), and
that his judge was to be the Lord Chief Justice, Sir George
Jefferys.

I have Sir Samuel's whole "Tryal and Conviction" before
me: it would take many pages to write it out, but portions
of it here and there will show what our forefathers had to
suffer in cruel mockings and gross injustice at the hands of
the notorious "Judge Jefferys."

THE TRIAL

There being an information against Sir Samuel Barnardiston for a very great misdemeanour, upon oath made that he
was so extremely indisposed that he could not appear in
person without danger of his life, the Court was pleased to
allow him the liberty of pleading by attorney (Mr. Williams).

Mr. Herbert: Your Lordship, one thing I would observe out of the last letter: "Great endeavours have been used to obtain his pardon, but the contrary party have carried it, which much dasheth our hopes." So it seems they have their hopes, and the writer of these letters a great share in them. We have, gentlemen, nothing to do but to prove that Sir Samuel Barnardiston was the author, writer and publisher of the letters, and we question not but to prove it clearly.

Mr. Williams: My Lord, he is indicted for writing and *publishing* these letters. A gentleman writes a letter to a private friend and sends it to the post-house; whether that be a publishing of a libel I leave it to your Lordship! And if there is no proof of the publication of them, I suppose, gentlemen, you will not take it upon your oaths that he is guilty. And I would know who they were directed to.

Judge Jefferys: Did he write them to keep them in his pocket do you think, Mr. Williams?

Mr. Williams: My Lord, is there any evidence of his *publishing* them? I see none. Things, too, are mentioned in the preamble, of which there is no proof, as that he is of a turbulent spirit.

Judge Jefferys: Why, Mr. Williams, would you have the jury find that he did it piously?

Mr. Williams: My Lord, there is a middle way.

Judge Jefferys: No, no! Mr. Williams; let us have none of your middle ways. Did he do it to serve the Crown? These letters are as base as the worst of mankind could have ever invented; the very thing is evidence of his malice, and let him give himself any fine name, by calling himself one of the sober party, or the godly party or the upright party, let him gild and paint himself as he pleaseth, the inside is rotten, factious and seditious, it shows venom and malice, malice against the king, government, church and state, indeed against all mankind not of the same persuasion as those miscreants. Here is a sanctifying of traitors!—"their party has prevailed"—as though for hanging traitors mankind must be divided into parties, and now our party, "the sober party," as he calls it, are in a sad condition. And here is the sainting of two horrid conspirators! it is high time for all mankind that have any christianity or sense of heaven, to bestir themselves to rid the nation of such caterpillars, such monsters of villany as these are. I am sure I may venture to call these venomous letters the borders of high treason itself. And now as to his *publishing* of them, of which Mr. Williams says there is no proof, is it not preposterous to think it should ever enter into any man's imagination, that he would write all this fustian stuff only to put it into his pocket? If you can believe this, upon my word you have a faith able to remove great mountains, but I assure you my faith cannot get to that strength. So, gentlemen, this information surely (if ever any was) is fully proved. Beware and know that these men that carry sheep's clothing and pretend zeal for religion, their insides are wolves and they are traitors in their minds.

Then the jury laid their heads together in the place where they stood, and the foreman gave in the verdict—Guilty.

If you have read "The Pilgrim's Progress" it may have struck you when reading the speech of Judge Jefferys that he took for his pattern Lord Hate-good, who said to Faithful, "Sirrah, sirrah, thou deservest to live no longer, but to be slain immediately upon the place." And indeed he was no better; he hated good and loved evil. But to his hatred he added injustice, and injustice is what the Bible, the Word of God, condemns in a judge more than anything. Sir Samuel was charged with publishing a libel against the king and government. To publish is to make a thing known to people in general, and as Mr. Williams said, Sir Samuel's letters were to a private friend. A libel is a malicious publication about a person tending to bring him into public scorn or hatred. Sir Samuel's letters contained no malice and were not published so the jurymen were wrong in giving the verdict "Guilty." But they were all cowards and knew that Jeffreys wanted them to give that unjust verdict.

'The Tryal' does not say what sentence the judge passed; it may have been imprisonment or a heavy fine. In giving parts of the speech I left out the low, bad, coarse swearing words the unjust judge used, but there was one little part which I will add. It was said of Jefferys that scarcely a day passed in court when he did not find fault with one or another of the lawyers who sat by, and he certainly did so in this case. When he was mocking and jeering at the expressions in the letters of Sir Samuel he said, "Nay, in these letters is the very language of that cursed traitor Walcot himself: 'raise up instruments'—'I am sorry for the death of our friend, honest Mr. Wright, but God Almighty can easily raise up instruments to do His work'—the very language of Walcot. And I would have you take notice of it, Mr. Blackerby; for I would have you take warning by these things" (speaking to a gentleman that was taking notes).

Mr. Blackerby: My lord, I have neither said nor done anything that should give you occasion to speak thus to me.

So there was one evidently who did not cringe to him as the jury did. "Mr. Blackerby"! surely we have heard the name before? Yes; the other story was about Mr. Blackerby the preacher, and his grandchildren who were brought up in Kedington, Squire Barnardiston's own village. The lawyer in court had most likely been a life-long friend of Sir Samuel; so here we have three upright men—Sir Samuel, Mr. Williams and Mr. Blackerby—among a host of unprincipled ones. And that was the very character of those times.

All through the reigns of the Stuart kings, the Puritans—strong Protestant Low Churchmen—the Baptists, the Independents and the Presbyterians suffered *outward* persecution, and at this time it was like the darkest night just before the

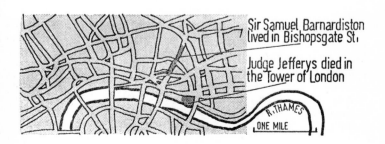

Sir Samuel Barnardiston lived in Bishopsgate St.

Judge Jefferys died in the Tower of London

R. THAMES

ONE MILE

dawn; five years more and the Protestant William III was to come to the throne and put an end to the High Church and Popish tyranny. And just as in the dark night the beasts of the forest creep forth, Judge Jefferys rose, and fell like a wolf upon the prey. His aim was to gain favour at Court— the most wicked Court England has ever had. During the Great Plague in 1665 when all was confusion, he appeared for the first time in a barrister's gown and some people said that he simply wore it without having won it. But he pleased the King so much that he rose step by step to be the chief judge in the land. He sentenced many scores of high-principled Protestants and patriotic people, aged, middle-aged and very young to death, and while doing so his features were distorted with rage and fury. He was the worst judge England has ever had. But the Word of God says: "If thou seest the oppression of the poor and violent perverting of judgment and justice in a province, marvel not at the matter, for He that is higher than the highest regardeth, and there be higher than they" (Eccles. 5.8). A change for the better will come in the end.

In December 1688, King James II left the kingdom, and Judge Jefferys knew that he would find no favour in the new Protestant court, so one dark morning he put on, not the red robe, but a shabby sailor's suit, and lurked about the docks some days; then one day, feeling unsafe, he went into a low alehouse and took his pot of beer to the cellar. But he found in that day when he went into the cellar to hide himself, that He that was higher than the highest regarded, and could "raise up instruments." A man who had once been at his bar, and who used to say that he would never forget the terrors of Jefferys' face, came in to see if a customer of his was there; he saw his former judge and went out and told who was there. Soon a mob of people crowded in, hurried him into a coach, the gathering crowds calling, "Vengeance! justice! justice!" He was taken first to the Lord Mayor and then to the Tower. There, he gave himself up to drink, and in three or four months died. Oh, that we may be saved from hating the righteous, for "they that hate the righteous shall be desolate!" (Psa. 34.21).

Reading all these interesting stories—and there are many more—makes us realise how wonderfully God has worked in days gone by: and He is just the same today. People today are proving that Jesus Christ can save them from their sins and the peace that pardoning love brings into the heart is indeed a *change for the better*. May you, dear reader, be brought to know 'this same Jesus' to the saving of the soul.